BARRON'S BOOK NOTES

VIRGIL'S
The Aeneid

BY

Kathleen O'Neill

SERIES EDITOR

Michael Spring
Editor, *Literary Cavalcade*
Scholastic Inc.

W9-BDX-724

BARRON'S EDUCATIONAL SERIES, INC.
Woodbury, New York / London / Toronto / Sydney

ACKNOWLEDGMENTS

We would like to acknowledge the many painstaking hours of work Holly Hughes and Thomas F. Hirsch have devoted to making the *Book Notes* series a success.

All inquiries should be addressed to:
Barron's Educational Series, Inc.
113 Crossways Park Drive
Woodbury, New York 11797

Library of Congress Catalog Card No. 84-18575

International Standard Book No. 0-8120-3400-7

Library of Congress Cataloging in Publication Data
O'Neill, Kathleen,
  Virgil's Aeneid.

  (Barron's book notes)
  Bibliography: p. 105
  Summary: A guide to reading "The Aeneid" with a critical and appreciative mind encouraging analysis of plot, style, form, and structure. Also includes background on the author's life, and times, sample tests, term paper suggestions, and a reading list.
  1. Virgil. Aeneis. [1. Virgil. Aeneis. 2. Classical literature—History and criticism] I. Title.
PA6826.05 1984   873'.01   84-18575
ISBN 0-8120-3400-7 (pbk.)

CONTENTS

ADVISORY BOARD

HOW TO USE THIS BOOK

You have to know how to approach literature in order to get the most out of it. This *Barron's Book Notes* volume follows a plan based on methods used by some of the best students to read a work of literature.

Begin with the guide's section on the author's life and times. As you read, try to form a clear picture of the author's personality, circumstances, and motives for writing the work. This background usually will make it easier for you to hear the author's tone of voice, and follow where the author is heading.

Then go over the rest of the introductory material—such sections as those on the plot, characters, setting, themes, and style of the work. Underline, or write down in your notebook, particular things to watch for, such as contrasts between characters and repeated literary devices. At this point, you may want to develop a system of symbols to use in marking your text as you read. (Of course, you should only mark up a book you own, not one that belongs to another person or a school.) Perhaps you will want to use a different letter for each character's name, a different number for each major theme of the book, a different color for each important symbol or literary device. Be prepared to mark up the pages of your book as you read. Put your marks in the margins so you can find them again easily.

Now comes the moment you've been waiting for—the time to start reading the work of literature. You may want to put aside your *Barron's Book Notes* volume until you've read the work all the way through. Or you may want to alternate, reading the *Book Notes* analysis of each section as soon as you have finished reading the corresponding part of the original. Before you move on, reread crucial passages you don't fully understand. (Don't take this guide's analysis for granted—make up your own mind as to what the work means.)

Once you've finished the whole work of literature, you may want to review it right away, so you can firm up your ideas about what it means. You may want to leaf through the book concentrating on passages you marked in reference to one character or one theme. This is also a good time to reread the *Book Notes* introductory material, which pulls together insights on specific topics.

When it comes time to prepare for a test or to write a paper, you'll already have formed ideas about the work. You'll be able to go back through it, refreshing your memory as to the author's exact words and perspective, so that you can support your opinions with evidence drawn straight from the work. Patterns will emerge, and ideas will fall into place; your essay question or term paper will almost write itself. Give yourself a dry run with one of the sample tests in the guide. These tests present both multiple-choice and essay questions. An accompanying section gives answers to the multiple-choice questions as well as suggestions for writing the essays. If you have to select a term paper topic, you may choose one from the list of suggestions in this book. This guide also provides you with a reading list, to help you when you start research for a term paper, and a selection of provocative comments by critics, to spark your thinking before you write.

THE AUTHOR AND HIS TIMES

Virgil (Publius Virgilius Maro) was born in Mantua, a rural town north of Rome near the Alps. Even though Virgil's birth in 70 B.C. came in the middle of a century of political turmoil and civil war in Rome, life in Mantua was relatively peaceful, and Virgil's father, who was a prosperous Roman citizen, could afford to give his son a good education in the basics, especially Greek and Roman literature. When Virgil was about 17, his father decided that he should be a politician, or possibly a businessman, and sent him to Rome to study rhetoric (the art of public speaking).

But Virgil was shy and hated having to make long, flowery speeches about things that didn't interest him at all. Instead he wrote poetry on the sly. His first and last attempt to argue a case in court was an embarrassing failure, and Virgil decided he didn't have a future in politics. He left Rome and went to live by the beautiful Bay of Naples where he studied philosophy.

This was probably a good idea because Roman politics could be dangerous, even fatal. The Roman Republic's government was collapsing in civil war and mobs often rioted in the streets. Rival generals brought their troops home from foreign wars and used them against each other, each one trying to rule Rome his own way. Then in 44 B.C. Julius Caesar, the great Roman dictator, was assassinated and Rome was plunged into its worst political crisis—one that lasted more than a decade.

Virgil was 26 years old at that time. Ever since his birth in 70 B.C. there had been nothing but this frightening chaos. He, and many other young men of his generation, were totally fed up with Roman politics. Virgil stayed in Naples and spent these years studying philosophy and writing poetry about the joys of country living. These poems, called the *Eclogues*, became an instant hit in Rome and were read aloud at fashionable dinner parties. By the age of 33, Virgil was rich and famous. Virgil followed up the *Eclogues* with the *Georgics*, a book of poems about farming.

Then in 31 B.C., something happened that completely changed Virgil's feelings about Rome and about what he wanted to write. The Emperor Augustus finally managed to end the civil wars that had plagued the city for so long and restored order and peace. For the first time in his life, Virgil had hope for the future of his country, and he felt deep gratitude and admiration for Augustus, the man who had made it all possible. Virgil was inspired to write his great epic poem, the *Aeneid*, to celebrate Rome and Augustus' achievement. He had come a long way from his early days writing about nature and hating politics.

Virgil was clever. He didn't just write a story about Augustus. He wanted to make Romans proud of their history and their vast empire. He also wanted to show how Augustus was the most recent in a long line of great Roman leaders—strong, dedicated to their city, and willing to make great sacrifices for it. So the very beginning of Virgil's poem tells how Aeneas and a small band of exiles traveled for years and fought bravely to build the city that would become Rome, the capital of the greatest empire in the world. As you read, you'll see that there are many parallels between what Aeneas does and what Augustus did. For example, Aeneas fights a civil war in Italy and finally puts

an end to the killing and chaos ...
did in Rome. You'll also see Aen...
beautiful African queen who resem... as Augustus
great Queen of Egypt, who marri...
(one of Augustus' rivals), and who als... with a
Augustus.

But the *Aeneid* is more than just a po...
about Rome. Like all great works of literatu...
universal meaning. In many ways Aeneas is...
search of himself and a new identity. In the b...
of the poem, he wishes that he could just sta...
and keep out of trouble but, by the end, he is ...
to do everything possible for the future of his pe...
You might see a parallel here comparable to Vir...
own wish, as a young man, to stay out of the politi...
uproar of Rome and his emergence as Rome's natio...
al poet.

As you read the *Aeneid* you'll also learn a lot about
Roman mythology, and about what Virgil believed
was the role of fate and the gods in men's lives. You'll
see that Virgil wasn't just out to praise Rome's
achievements. He believed that Rome and Augustus
were destined to rule the world. However, he also
worried about the people who got in the way of that
destiny, often through no fault of their own. Some of
the characters you might like best are those, like Dido
and Turnus, who are hurt by Aeneas' triumphs. Virgil's own experience of the horrors of civil war made
him understand that there are always good and bad
on both sides of any conflict.

You're going to see that Virgil was a great writer
and a superb storyteller. You'll read about terrifying
dangers, great battles, and even a passionate
romance. (For a short time, when Virgil was young,
he was a soldier. His vivid descriptions of war prove
that he had had firsthand experience.) You'll also see

The Autho

Virgil's early love
tions of the sea
Virgil wor
epic poem
and his
which
E o
illing
ople.
gil's
cal

re in his beautiful descrip-
countryside.
Aeneid for eleven years. This
great skill and care in writing,
knowledge of Greek literature,
d ever since he was a boy. The
knew about the project and asked
while it was in progress. Of course
Virgil was 51 years old, in 19 B.C.,
Greece to visit some of the places
ited. He got very sick, and Augustus
ck to Italy where he died. Virgil told
rn the Aeneid because there were still
to rewrite. Fortunately, Augustus
the Aeneid was saved. It became
nal epic almost immediately and is now
one of the greatest works of Western liter-

THE POEM

The Plot

For seven years, a great warrior named Aeneas leads a small band of fellow Trojans around the Mediterranean, looking for a place to build a new city. They were exiled from the city of Troy when the Greeks conquered it and burned it to the ground. Fate has decreed that they will be the founders of Rome, but they are having a hard time getting there.

A goddess named Juno, hates them and will do anything to prevent them from reaching Italy. They are almost there when she whips up a great storm that blows them off course. They end up in Africa, at a city named Carthage, which is Juno's favorite city. Carthage is ruled by Queen Dido, who is beautiful and kind. She welcomes them to Carthage and invites them to a great banquet.

At the banquet, Aeneas tells Dido his whole sad story. First, he describes how the Greeks finally conquered Troy by hiding inside a giant wooden horse and tricking the Trojans into pulling it into the city. He then tells how his mother, a goddess named Venus, warned him to flee, and told him that he was fated to establish a new city for his people. Even though Aeneas would rather have died fighting for Troy, he obeys the goddess and follows his fate. He carries his aging father, Anchises, on his shoulders and holds his little son, Ascanius, by the hand. His wife dies at Troy.

Aeneas tells Dido how he and the other Trojan exiles built a small fleet and began sailing around the Mediterranean looking for their new home. But they misunderstand omens that tell where the new city will be, and they keep trying to settle in the wrong place. Each time some disaster strikes, forcing them to move on again. Along the way, Aeneas suffers another tragedy when his father dies. Aeneas finishes his story by telling Dido that the Trojans had just figured out that they were supposed to go to the west coast of Italy to build their new city when Juno's storm carried them to Carthage.

Meanwhile Aeneas' mother, Venus, is so worried that Juno may make Dido turn against Aeneas that she makes Dido fall passionately in love with him. Dido is so infatuated with Aeneas that she completely forgets about her reputation and her kingdom. For a year, Aeneas, forgetting all about Italy, stays happily with Dido. But then, Jupiter, the king of the gods, scolds him for neglecting his fate and the future of his country. Aeneas, who always obeys the gods and does what's best for his country, immediately leaves for Italy. Dido, wild with grief and anger, accuses him of betraying her. When Aeneas answers only that he must obey the gods, Dido kills herself in despair.

After leaving Carthage, the Trojans stop in Sicily and honor the anniversary of Anchises' death with great funeral games. Finally, the Trojans get to Italy and Aeneas takes a magical trip to the underworld to visit his father. Anchises shows him the glorious future that lies ahead for the Roman Empire, and Aeneas sees a parade of great statesmen and generals who will be born in the future. Until this time, Aeneas has been doing what fate and the gods command. Now, for the first time, he's really inspired by the future of his new city and he stops wishing he were back at Troy.

But the Trojans still have plenty of trouble ahead in Italy. When they first land near the site of what will be

Rome, Latinus, the king of the native Latins, welcomes them, and tells Aeneas that he is destined to marry Latinus' daughter, Lavinia, and to start a great new race from the mingling of Latin and Trojan blood.

Juno is still furious at the Trojans, however. Although she knows that Aeneas is fated to build his new city and to marry Lavinia, she can delay those events and make the Trojans pay heavily for them. She sends an evil goddess, Allecto, to poison the Latins' minds against the Trojans. In particular, Allecto infects a warrior named Turnus with an uncontrollable passion for war. He had planned to marry Lavinia himself.

At first, the Trojans are outnumbered and Aeneas goes to get help from other cities, including one that is built on the exact spot where Rome would later be built. When he returns, there are many ferocious battles between the Latins and the Trojans. Finally, to stop the needless bloodshed, Aeneas challenges Turnus to fight him alone. After some delays caused by Juno, the two great warriors meet. In the final scene Aeneas wounds Turnus and Turnus admits that he was wrong. Nevertheless, Aeneas kills him, either out of anger or as justified punishment for all the violence Turnus has caused.

The Characters

Aeneas

Aeneas is a great survivor. He's one of those people who can lose everything and still start over again. He goes from being a victim of the Greeks at Troy to becoming a conqueror in Italy. He starts out as an unhappy and unwilling exile and becomes the founder of a great city. Aeneas is the first hero in Western literature who changes and develops. His struggles help him discover who he is and what he thinks is important.

Is Aeneas great because his fate made him great or is he great because he had the courage and determination to live up to the role fate handed him? There is a side to Aeneas—particularly in the first four books of the *Aeneid*—that isn't very impressive, even if you can understand why he feels the way he does. He's sad, tired, always waiting for his father or the gods to tell him what to do. But Aeneas always fulfills his duty to his family, to his country, and to the gods, even when he's depressed. He is never selfish. He always puts his responsibility to others first. If you have to name one quality that defines Aeneas, it is this devotion to duty, a quality the Romans called *pietas* or piety. This quality keeps him going even when he would rather forget about his fate. Ultimately, this same quality makes him accept, even welcome, that fate. Because, when Aeneas finally realizes that all his efforts will make the glorious Roman Empire possible, his love of his family and his country are fulfilled. The result is that the Aeneas you see at the end of the *Aeneid* is determined, sure of himself and confident that he knows what's right. He has become a great leader who is able to impose order on people who display more selfish and unruly emotions.

Aeneas achieves his self-control at a stiff price to himself and, often, to others. He leaves Dido, a woman who rescued him and his Trojans and who loves him deeply, with no explanation except that he must follow his fate to Italy. You may decide that he's a cold-blooded achiever. Or you may decide that Aeneas felt terrible pain at leaving Dido and was able to leave only through the heroic mastery of his feelings. Aeneas is a great warrior, able and willing to brutally kill his enemies, but he is often horrified by death. Even in the last scene of the *Aeneid*, where Aeneas kills his most bitter rival, Turnus, you see that he has a moment of pity.

Aeneas does not just live in the moment. He lives with a strong sense of history. He remembers his past in Troy and he sees the future in store for his people. Aeneas' own life shows the terrible price men pay to build great civilizations. He has to suppress his own feelings in order to bring order. Some readers also see Aeneas as a link between the classical world of heroes, which admired strong but often selfish individuals, and the later Christian era with its greater emphasis on compassion for other people.

Aeneas would not be great at a party. He never cracks jokes. His complete devotion to duty can be a little dull. Virgil may have made him this way, in part, because Aeneas was supposed to represent Augustus, who was a very reserved, even cold, person. Another reason that Aeneas may not seem like a real person is that Virgil didn't want you to think of him that way. After all, Aeneas is the son of a goddess. He is partly divine or partly a myth himself. Aeneas is larger than life. Virgil turned him into a model of a great leader—firm, stern, but compassionate. He is a symbol of the great Roman virtues of duty and leadership.

Dido

Of all the characters in the *Aeneid*, Dido is probably the one you might relate to most. She's the most human. She's beautiful, generous, kind, and successful. She has strong emotions. She's the queen of a bustling city, Carthage. When you first see her, she offers a welcome relief from Aeneas' endless problems. But she ends up killing herself. What goes wrong?

On the simplest level, Dido's story is the classic story of unrequited love. She loves Aeneas more than he loves her. For a year they have a passionate affair and everything is great. But then Aeneas decides he has to leave. His respect for the gods and his duty to his people are stronger than his love. But nothing is more important to Dido than her love for Aeneas. She burns with love. She is totally distracted. When Aeneas finally leaves, she becomes alternately bitter, vindictive, and pathetic, as she curses Aeneas and then begs him to stay. She is a victim of uncontrolled passion.

Where did this passion come from? Is it Cupid's fault for wounding her with his arrow? If so, then what happens to Dido is not her fault. She's the victim of the gods and of Aeneas' fate to go to Italy. Part of Virgil's theme here is simply that life is terribly unfair to some people. Virgil wants you to feel sorry for Dido. After all, she got a raw deal.

But is there more to it? Do you really believe that Cupid was entirely to blame or was Dido ready to fall in love? Is passion part of her nature? The first time we see her we see that she is an extremist. She wants to stay up all night to hear Aeneas' story. Her vow never to remarry after her first husband died also seems a little drastic. Even her sister Anna thinks so.

Whatever started it, this excessive passion destroys Dido. For one thing, it makes her irrational. Aeneas' story should have warned her that he would eventually leave for Italy. A more rational person would at least have asked him what his plans were. Instead,

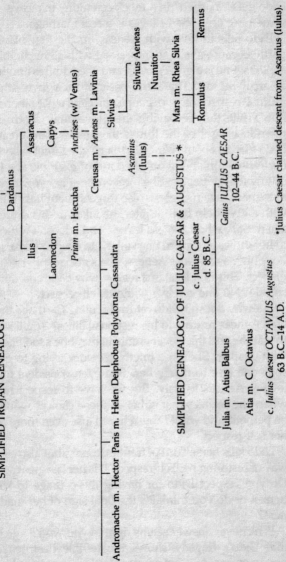

SIMPLIFIED TROJAN GENEALOGY

Teucer
Dardanus

Ilus — Assaracus
Laomedon — Capys
Priam m. Hecuba — Anchises (w/ Venus)
Creusa m. Aeneas m. Lavinia

Andromache m. Hector Paris m. Helen Deiphobus Polydorus Cassandra

Ascanius (Iulus) - - - - - - - - -

Silvius
Silvius Aeneas
Numitor

Mars m. Rhea Silvia

Romulus   Remus

SIMPLIFIED GENEALOGY OF JULIUS CAESAR & AUGUSTUS *

Gaius JULIUS CAESAR
102–44 B.C.

c. Julius Caesar
d. 85 B.C.

Julia m. Atius Balbus

Atia m. C. Octavius

c. Julius Caesar OCTAVIUS Augustus
63 B.C.–14 A.D.

*Julius Caesar claimed descent from Ascanius (Iulus).

Dido gets "married" in a mock ceremony in a cave—
something only she believes is a real marriage.

Dido falls in love with Aeneas, in the first place,
partly because she is so impressed with all his heroic
exploits. She is a great person and she admires another great person. That's the basis of their love—the
mutual respect of two people in similar situations.
But, while they're having their love affair, both of
them lose sight of the things that made them great.
Dido forgets about ruling Carthage; she forgets about
her reputation and about the kind of example she is
setting for her people. She forgets about her vow never to marry again. Aeneas also forgets about Italy but,
with a little help from Jupiter, he takes up his duties
again. Still, when Aeneas leaves, Dido doesn't return
to her duties as queen. She sinks into despair because
not only has she lost Aeneas, she's also lost her self-
respect. This is at least one reason why Dido commits
suicide. No one can live without self-respect.

But why doesn't Dido return to ruling Carthage the
way Aeneas returns to his responsibilities? You'll see
that at the end this never occurs to her. She's too filled
with despair. She does briefly consider trying to get
someone else to marry her. She even considers following Aeneas to Italy. But we have to respect her
when she realizes that either of these choices would
be pathetic and would cause her to lose even more of
her self-respect.

Dido kills herself out of frantic despair, but also as a
way of restoring her self-respect. It is her last great act.
Do you respect Dido for having the courage to kill
herself or do you think it's the final sign of her madness?

Whichever answer seems right to you, you'll agree
that Dido's tragedy shows the terrible destructive
power of uncontrolled passion. In this way she is like

Juno and Turnus but, in another way, she is totally different. They are angry and violent, lashing out at others, but Dido is ruined by love. In the end, she does curse Aeneas and predict a great war between Carthage and Rome, but Dido never actually hurts anyone but herself, and this makes her tragedy the greatest in the *Aeneid*.

Turnus

Turnus is a daredevil. If he were alive today, he might be the person who drag-races on Main Street at 3:00 A.M. to show off. He's incredibly competitive. He may not care that much about what he's fighting for, but he's proud of being a great warrior and he isn't going to let anyone get ahead of him.

Turnus isn't a nasty person. He doesn't really mean to cause as much harm as he does. Because he never really stops to think about the consequences of his actions, everything he does is incredibly destructive. That's why Virgil always compares him to a wild animal.

And that's Turnus' great flaw. You'll see that Virgil is no pacifist. He thinks that war and killing can be justified. He does not criticize Aeneas for fighting for his people and their right to make a home in Italy. But Turnus is mostly fighting for himself. Turnus never considers the possibility of a reasonable compromise with the Trojans. Even after his allies want to make peace, Turnus cannot stop fighting.

But is Turnus to blame for this? Literally, the story tells you that Turnus is set on fire with lust for war by Allecto's blazing torch. Is this passion something that Turnus couldn't help? Or was it in his personality all along; and is Allecto only a symbol for why it heated up? (This is the same question we asked about Dido and Cupid.)

You might think that the second answer sounds more reasonable. We no longer believe that evil goddesses like Allecto really exist. But there is another way of thinking about whether or not Turnus is to blame. In some ways he is just defending his country from invasion by a foreign army, the Trojans. What is wrong with that? What would your reaction be if a foreign army arrived in the United States and said, "Oh, by the way, we're here because the fates told us to come"? If you think about it that way, what Turnus does is perfectly reasonable, and he's innocent because he has no way of knowing that Aeneas really is right about his fate. He doesn't know that Aeneas will win. If he could have known that in advance, of course there would have been no reason to fight. But he can't know that Aeneas will win until close to the end. To his credit, when Aeneas is about to kill him, he realizes that he was wrong and admits it.

You get an interesting insight into Juno when you think about Turnus this way. One of the things wrong with Juno is that she keeps fighting fate. That's irrational on her part because she knows what the fates have in store. But Turnus really doesn't know. So what is evil in Juno becomes tragic in Turnus. He's doing the best he can but he doesn't realize that he's on the losing end of history.

You can also compare Turnus to Dido. They are both victims of uncontrolled passion and of Aeneas and his fate. Dido's misfortune is that she lives in a country where Aeneas isn't meant to stay. Turnus' problem is that he lives in a country where Aeneas is supposed to stay. But Dido harms only herself while Turnus kills many innocent people. And that makes a big difference. Dido is purely tragic, but it's hard to know exactly what to feel about Turnus.

Still another way of looking at Turnus is that he is the old-fashioned hero, the rugged individualist, who can never accept any authority other than his own. He cannot live in a peaceful, civilized state like the new order that Aeneas will start. There is no place for people like Turnus in Rome because they're the kind of people who start civil wars.

Juno

If you're really unlucky you may have met someone like Juno. She could be a distant relative who comes to the annual family reunion hopelessly overdressed and wants you to tell her how great she looks. You have to flatter her or she'll pester you all evening. She remembers all insults—real or imagined—and she talks about them for hours. She can't imagine what she ever did to deserve such disrespect. When the party's over, she still insists that no one paid any attention to her.

But Juno's even worse than this because she's a real troublemaker. She doesn't just talk about how angry she is, she acts on it. Since she's a goddess (and married to Jupiter) she can cause big trouble. If she wants a storm she can get it, and when she wants an evil demon, like Allecto, to drive people crazy all she has to do is call. Juno never controls her feelings. She simply lets everything out—and it's all bad.

The strangest thing is that Juno, despite her ruthlessness, never gets what she wants. Have you ever noticed how true that is about angry people? They just go from one fight to another, but they never seem to win. Why is that? One reason is that they are often irrational. They pick fights they can't win. They're also very self-destructive. They're so angry that they don't realize that their plans will backfire and produce exactly what they don't want. A good example of this is Juno's invention of a mock marriage between Dido and Aeneas in order to force Aeneas to stay in Carthage. Aeneas leaves anyway and Dido's life is ruined.

Why is Juno so angry at the Trojans? She has one petty reason—she lost a beauty contest—and one good reason. Carthage is Juno's favorite city and Rome (which the Trojans will found) is destined to destroy Carthage. That sounds like a rather good reason to be furious, and it is. However, no one, not even Juno, can change that destiny. It's inevitable. It's a part of fate and in Virgil's world even the gods can't change fate. So, in fighting fate, Juno is doing something basically irrational. She's fighting a battle she can never win. All she can do is make trouble.

This gives you a clue to what Juno symbolizes in the *Aeneid*. She is a force for disorder. Her uncontrolled rage does nothing but cause misery and death. Her weapons are found in nature: storms and fire on one hand, passions in men on the other. Thus, one way you can view Juno is as a symbol of violent and destructive forces that are always present in the world.

Juno will never stop on her own, but after her anger has burned itself out a bit, she will obey a command to stop from a god more powerful than she. That's Jupiter, her husband and the king of the gods. Similarly, you'll see that the effects of her rage on men like Turnus can eventually be controlled by other men, like Aeneas, who are strong enough to impose order.

Venus

The goddess Venus is Aeneas' mother. Like all mothers, she would like to see her son succeed. In fact, she wants him to succeed so much that she doesn't really care how hard it may be on him. For example, Venus agrees with Juno's scheme to have Dido and Aeneas marry in a mock ceremony. Venus doesn't care because she knows that Aeneas will have to leave anyway. But she doesn't stop to think about Aeneas' feelings when he has to leave. Venus isn't very warm. She's not interested in having long chats with her son, and she enjoys tricking him by disguising herself.

Like Juno, Venus loves to intervene in human affairs and helps Aeneas out of several difficult spots, but like Juno she can't change the basic course of fate. All she does is restore the balance after Juno has tipped it against Aeneas. But Venus' actions never restore order; in fact, they sometimes make matters worse. She's just another competing force against Juno. While she's not angry and destructive like Juno, she's not particularly admirable, either. Basically, Venus is concerned only about what she wants. If people like Dido get hurt in the process, Venus doesn't care.

In Roman mythology Venus was the goddess of love. It's no accident that she's Aeneas' mother. After all doesn't his great sense of responsibility come from his love of his family and country? But in Virgil's world you also see that love isn't necessarily as positive an emotion as we think it is today. Venus is responsible for Dido's uncontrollable passion. And Venus herself seems to be more a goddess of self-interest than one of true love and generosity.

Jupiter

Jupiter is the only god in the *Aeneid* who acts the way you would think a god should. He's calm, rational, impartial. But in one way he's very different from

what you would think a god should be. He's not particularly interested in goodness. His major interest is
to see that everything goes according to fate. As a
result he, unlike Juno and Venus, tends not to intervene unless things get seriously out of control.

Jupiter is the only god who really has the power to
change things. For example, he can stop Juno from
making trouble. He doesn't simply try to foil her the
way Venus does. In some ways you might decide that
there really is only one god, Jupiter, in the *Aeneid* and
that the other gods are just symbols of natural and
human forces.

You may ask why Jupiter doesn't intervene sooner
and stop Juno from her futile but destructive efforts to
change fate and prevent Aeneas from reaching Italy.
If you think of Jupiter as a personality instead of a
god, it's easy to understand why. He's married to
Juno and has learned to indulge her a bit. It's easier for
him to let her defuse her anger on the Trojans than to
have her raging around him all day. But even if you
view Jupiter as a god, his delay suggests that he himself is also a part of nature. He represents a basic force
toward order but other chaotic forces also exist (like
Juno) and he must let them run their course. Jupiter
and the forces of order may ultimately win, but there
may have to be a thunderstorm before the sky clears.
Juno has to rant and rave for a while before her anger
can abate.

Virgil also uses Jupiter as a way of giving official and
religious approval to the Roman Empire. When Jupiter predicts that the Roman Empire will reach the stars
and that it will last forever, Romans of Virgil's day
must have felt that their power over the world was
not only right but inevitable.

Anchises

Anchises is Aeneas' father. When you first meet him, he is an old man, stubbornly refusing to budge from burning Troy. That's where he's lived his life; that's where he's going to die. Only after he sees two impressive omens, which say that his grandson is destined for great things, is he willing to go. Aeneas carries him out of the city on his shoulders.

Anchises is literally and symbolically a burden to Aeneas. Aeneas loves and respects his father very much. But Anchises is basically rooted in the past, even though he becomes a fervent supporter of the Trojans' search for a new city. Anchises makes mistakes—he sends the Trojans to Crete, which is relatively near Troy, instead of sending them to Italy. This shows that Anchises can't think radically. He's not up to a big change. He's naïve. He thinks that the future will resemble the past. His naïveté is shown by the fact that, unlike Aeneas, he doesn't seem to worry that much. He doesn't have doubts about the future. Anchises must die and go to the underworld before he will understand how different the future will be. Anchises symbolizes the old life and the old ways of Troy. Aeneas loves and respects these things, just as he loves and respects his father, but he must leave them behind and go on alone to find a totally new life in Italy. Anchises' death symbolizes that he remains a Trojan, a man of an earlier era.

Latinus

Latinus, king of the Latins, is the first native king Aeneas meets in Italy. Latinus has heard many omens that his daughter Lavinia is destined to marry a stranger, and that together they will start a new race that will rule the world. So Latinus is well disposed toward Aeneas when Aeneas first arrives.

But Latinus has not reckoned with the fact that his people are opposed to sharing their kingdom with strangers. He completely overlooks the problems that will arise from his refusal to let Turnus marry Lavinia, as he had planned to do. Even though Latinus wants to do what is in line with fate, and his wish to welcome Aeneas to Latium is a rational act, he does not have the authority to enforce his wishes. He can't even explain his plans convincingly to his wife. Finally, he allows himself to be bullied into making war against the Trojans.

Latinus is an old man who has lost most of his power. You can see him as a real person and feel sorry for the terrible trap he is in, but you can also see him as a symbol of the weakness of the Latin society before Aeneas' arrival. Latinus' inability to control his people strongly suggests that the Latin people needed a new leader. This fact helps Virgil justify or overlook the fact that the Trojans were invaders of Italy.

Latinus can also be compared with other senior citizens in the *Aeneid*. Like Priam, the king of Troy right before the Greeks destroyed it, he makes fatal mistakes that lead to the fall of his city. He also resembles Anchises because he wishes for the right things but he doesn't know how to attain them. Just as Priam and Anchises belonged to the old world of Troy—a world that must die—so Latinus belongs to the old world of Italy—one that must die to make room for Rome and its new order.

Evander

Evander is a very symbolic character. His city, Pallanteum, is on the exact spot where Rome will be built. Evander illustrates some of the qualities that the

Romans were particularly proud of. Pallanteum and
its king are simple and rustic, without finery or luxury
of any kind. You know that Americans admire the
pioneers for being able to survive in the wilderness.
The Romans liked to think that they had these same
types of people in their background, too. When
Aeneas sleeps on a bed of leaves in Evander's tiny
hut, he shows that he has given up the old luxuries
that he may have enjoyed in Troy or in Carthage with
Dido.

Evander also becomes a substitute father figure,
replacing Anchises. Aeneas treats him with great
respect and his family loyalty is transferred to a father
with roots in Italy. Evander also shows the greatest of
Roman virtues: good political judgment. He knows
how and where Aeneas can find allies.

Other Elements

SETTING

The *Aeneid* is set in the middle of the 12th century
B.C. after the fall of Troy. Troy was in Asia Minor, in
what is now Turkey. In Book II you see how Troy,
which was a wealthy, fortified city filled with temples
and palaces, is destroyed by the Greeks. The first six
books of the *Aeneid* describe how Aeneas and a small
band of Trojans are forced to flee Troy. They spend
more than seven years sailing around the Mediterranean Sea in primitive wooden boats trying to find Italy. Finally, after many detours and disasters, they
arrive on the west coast of Italy. (For a map of
Aeneas's wanderings, see page 45.)

The Trojans land at the mouth of the Tiber, the

same river that flows through present-day Rome. When the Trojans arrive, there are several small, simple cities (nothing like Troy) in the surrounding countryside, which is called Latium. At first the king of the biggest city, Laurentium, is willing to share his land with the Trojans, but soon his people rebel and band together with the people of the other cities to drive the Trojans away. The Trojans, led by Aeneas, battle them and finally succeed in capturing Laurentium, just as the Greeks had once captured Troy. After the war ends, the Trojans and the native people of Italy (including the Latins, Etruscans, and Rutulians) will live together and intermarry, becoming the ancestors of the Romans.

According to tradition, Troy fell in 1184 B.C. and Rome was founded in 753 B.C. Thus, more than 400 years passed between Aeneas' landing at the Tiber and the founding of Rome. Virgil explains part of this time gap in Book I. After the war, Aeneas will build a city called Lavinium and rule there for three years. His son Ascanius will move the city to nearby Alba Longa and rule for thirty years. His descendants will rule for 300 years after that until Romulus builds the walls around Rome. If you do some quick figuring, you'll realize that this leaves about 100 years unaccounted for. The reason for this may be that Virgil thought Troy fell at a later date than we do, or it may be that Virgil was less concerned with exact historical accuracy than he was with creating a poetic and almost mythological story of Rome's beginnings.

THEMES

The *Aeneid* has many themes, which you'll see as you go through The Story section of this guide. There are many different ways to consider the poem's meaning because Virgil's story works on several different levels. For example, the *Aeneid* tells the history of Rome, but it also tells the personal story of its hero, Aeneas. To help you understand these levels, here is a list of the major themes you should focus on:

1. THE *AENEID* IS A NATIONAL EPIC ABOUT THE BEGINNING OF ROME

Virgil's poem tells how Rome came to be in historical and symbolic terms. The story blends history and myth to show how and why the Trojans reached Italy, and how Rome began. Virgil also explains the forces that made Rome great: fate and great courage, determination, and selflessness on the part of its first leader, Aeneas. Aeneas symbolizes the virtues that allowed the Romans to build a great empire.

2. THE *AENEID* IS A TRIBUTE TO AUGUSTUS AND A CELEBRATION OF THE END OF THE CIVIL WARS IN ROME

Aeneas is the model of a great leader. Virgil meant you to see him as a symbol for the Emperor Augustus. The wars between the Latins and the Trojans, which Virgil describes in the *Aeneid*, can be compared to the civil wars that raged in Rome before Augustus took control. When Aeneas defeats Turnus and ends the disorder that Turnus created, he is similar to Augustus, who ended the conflict between the warring factions in Rome.

3. THE *AENEID* IS THE STORY OF AENEAS' PERSONAL SEARCH FOR A NEW IDENTITY

Aeneas changes from a lost and lonely exile with no idea of his destination to a determined, self-confident leader. He gives up his past, as represented by Troy, and accepts the future, as represented by Rome. In the process of becoming a great leader he makes many personal sacrifices, including giving up Dido's love. He is completely devoted to his family and country, and never wavers from these duties, but he also understands the terrible price that others, like Turnus, have to pay for Aeneas' success. This ability to understand and to feel sorry for other people is what makes him such a great character. He's not just a simple-minded hero; he has a heart.

4. THE *AENEID* DESCRIBES THE STRUGGLE BETWEEN THE FORCES OF ORDER AND DISORDER IN THE WORLD

Virgil's world is a harsh one. The forces of disorder are always present. They are symbolized by Juno's uncontrollable rage at the Trojans and by the irrational passions that Dido and Turnus feel. These forces always lead to death and destruction.

Ultimately, though, Virgil seems to be saying that fate is on the side of order. Jupiter, the king of the gods and a force for order, finally tells Juno to stop making trouble. Aeneas, also a force for order because of his tremendous sense of duty and self-sacrifice, brings order to Italy.

5. THE *AENEID* DESCRIBES THE RELATIONSHIP BETWEEN PEOPLE AND FATE

A person's life depends on his fate, something even the gods cannot change. Fate isn't fair—Dido and Turnus have tragic fates, even though they may not have done anything wrong. But someone's fate may also reflect the kind of person involved. Aeneas' responsibility to his country makes him a great leader, and he is fated to succeed. Dido and Turnus have excessively passionate natures that lead to their downfalls. Virgil seems to be saying that your fate is a combination of luck (which you can't control) and your own personality (which perhaps you can).

FORM AND STRUCTURE

The *Aeneid* is an epic poem written in 12 books. An epic poem is a long, narrative poem about the adventures of a great hero. Virgil's *Aeneid* is modeled in part on the great Greek epic poems, the *Iliad* and the *Odyssey*, by Homer. The *Iliad* describes the exploits of Achilles and other Greek heroes in the Trojan War (the same war that forced Aeneas to leave Troy and that is described in Book II of the Aeneid). The *Odyssey* describes how Ulysses (or Odysseus in Greek) wandered for many years, trying to return home after the Trojan War.

The first six books of the *Aeneid* parallel the *Odyssey* because they describe Aeneas' search for a home. Aeneas even stops in many of the same places that Ulysses did. There is an important difference, however. Ulysses was trying to find his old home, while Aeneas is searching for a new home.

The second six books parallel the *Iliad*. They describe the war in Italy just as the Iliad describes the Trojan War. Again, there are many parallels. For example, the Trojans are besieged inside their fort in Italy just as they were trapped inside Troy. But again there is an important difference. The *Iliad* describes how the Trojans lost the war and Troy fell. In the *Aeneid* the Trojans win the war in Italy and get the chance to build a new city.

Virgil imitates many scenes from the *Iliad* and the *Odyssey* in his epic, but he always changes them in significant ways so that they illustrate his own Roman themes. One of the most important differences between Homer's epics and the *Aeneid* is that the *Aeneid* is a patriotic poem while the *Iliad* and the *Odyssey* are poems about individuals and their adventures. Homer emphasizes heroes, not countries. But one of

Virgil's main points is to show how Rome became the city it is, and to show what kind of person makes a good Roman citizen and leader.

You can also think about the *Aeneid* as being divided into three parts. The first four books take place with Dido in Carthage, including a flashback to the fall of Troy. The second four books (V–VIII) describe the Trojans' arrival in Italy and Aeneas' trip to the underworld where he sees the future of Rome. The last four books (IX–XII) describe the war in Italy and Aeneas' triumph over Turnus.

You can also consider the books of the *Aeneid* in pairs. The odd-numbered books tend to be less dramatic (for example, Book III in which the Trojans' wanderings are described or Book V where the funeral games for Anchises are shown). The even-numbered books reach more emotional peaks of tragedy or glory (for example, the death of Dido in Book IV, and Aeneas' vision of the future in Book VI).

STYLE

Just as the *Aeneid*'s structure is modeled in part on the *Iliad* and the *Odyssey*, so is its style. Like Homer, Virgil wrote his poem in *dactyllic hexameter*. This term describes the meter or rhythm of each line of poetry. It means that there are six major beats in each line and that each beat is made up of a *dactyl* (a word in which the first syllable is strong and the following two are weak) (–ˇˇ) and a *spondee* (a word in which both syllables are long (––). An example of a dactyl and a spondee in English are the words "fabulous pizza!". Of course, since you are reading the *Aeneid* in an English translation, what you're reading won't have this rhythm. But it's interesting to try to imagine how musical it must have sounded in the original Latin.

The reason for this rhythm is that Homer's epics were sung or chanted before they were written down, so it was natural to have a clear beat. Virgil kept this rhythm, even though he wrote his poem for a literate and sophisticated audience. But since he *wrote* the poem, instead of learning it from an oral tradition, he had the opportunity to use much more complex language than Homer could have. Virgil's poem is full of beautiful images, subtle allusions, and symbolism that give it a rich, dense texture. The result is that Virgil's epic has a very different style from Homer's.

Virgil also follows epic tradition in using many *epic similes* and *epithets*. An example of an *epic simile* is found in Book IV where Virgil compares Aeneas to a giant oak tree that cannot be blown down no matter how hard the winds blow. An *epithet* is a stock phrase that captures some part of a person's basic character. An example is "pious" Aeneas. The epithets you'll see depend on which translation you're using. Just look for the same word used over and over again to describe a person.

Another epic convention that Virgil makes great use of is long speeches by the major characters. Here we see that Virgil finally made use of his training in rhetoric. Although he might not have been a good public speaker himself, his characters surely are.

POINT OF VIEW

Except for Books II and III where Aeneas tells his own story, the *Aeneid* is told from the point of view of an all-knowing narrator. This narrator is of course Virgil, but he pretends to get all his information from a goddess called the Muse. (If you look at the very beginning of the *Aeneid*, you'll see where Virgil asks the Muse for help in telling the story.) By following this convention of epic poetry, Virgil implies that his poem is accurate and objective. For example, when he says that Jupiter predicts that the Romans will rule forever, we're supposed to believe that he's right because the Muse told him it was true.

In reality the *Aeneid* is a very subjective poem. For one, you already know that one of the things Virgil wanted to do was to praise Augustus and the Roman Empire. That's not objective at all, but reflects Virgil's own beliefs. Even more importantly, Virgil has an unusual ability to get inside his characters' heads. For example, even though Dido seems to be described from the outside, you know exactly how she feels and what she's thinking about. The result is that you feel that you know her, and you feel very sorry for her.

Perhaps most important is Virgil's combination of an objective and subjective point of view that allows you to see Aeneas' character both from the outside and from the inside. For example, in Book IV when Aeneas leaves Dido, you see him almost from Dido's point of view. He hardly says anything to defend himself, and you get very little indication of his own feelings. This may make you dislike Aeneas a bit, but it also makes you see how much of his own feelings must be sacrificed in order to found Rome. By using this "outside" point of view, Virgil suggests that in some ways Aeneas' feelings don't matter that much. The important thing is that he does his duty.

But if that were the only side of Aeneas you see, he wouldn't be very interesting. So Virgil sometimes shows you things from Aeneas' "inside" point of view. For example, in Book I, when he is hit by Juno's storm and cries out that he wishes he had died in Troy, you learn what an unhappy and unwilling traveler he is at this point. Books II and III are told almost

entirely from Aeneas' point of view and that's where
you learn the most about him. If you think about it,
you'll notice that much of the story in the early books
of the *Aeneid* is told from Aeneas' point of view. This
becomes less and less true later on. This shift in point
of view reflects the change in Aeneas himself from an
uncertain exile to a great leader. Virgil seems to be
saying that as Aeneas learns to accept his great fate,
he has fewer internal conflicts that you as the reader
need to see. It may also be that as Aeneas becomes a
great leader he can't afford to let whatever conflicts he
does have show. As a result, this shift in point of view
makes Aeneas into more of a myth—a model of a
great leader—and less of an ordinary person.

The Story

BOOK I

Imagine this scene: It's around 1150 B.C. Seven
years earlier, a band of fierce Greek warriors invaded
the city of Troy and set it on fire. Aeneas and a few
fellow Trojans manage to escape to the coast where
they launch their wooden boats and set sail to the
west. There, some fortune-tellers have said, they will
find a new home. They've been wandering all over
the sea ever since, looking for this place.

When we first see him, Aeneas is filled with con-
flicting emotions. One part of him is still grieving for
his lost city and all the friends and family who died
there. Another part of him is worn out with troubles
and worries about whether or not he will ever find a
place where his people can settle. But, for the

moment, he is simply relieved that the sun is shining
and the sea is calm. He's beginning to have a little
hope again. He does not suspect that an angry goddess is watching, and that she is determined to make
as much trouble as possible for him and his fellow
Trojans, wherever they go.

This is the moment Virgil picks to start his story of
Aeneas' struggles to establish a new city—the city
that would eventually become Rome, the capital of
the Roman Empire and the greatest city in the
world.

NOTE: The events in the *Aeneid* are not told in
chronological order. You will see that Books II and III
will take you back in time to the fall of Troy, while
Book VI will show the future of Rome after Aeneas.
Keep this blending of past, present, and future in
mind as you read.

Before the action starts, Virgil tells us what his
poem is about. The short prologue gives us many
clues about the major themes, so it's worth reading
carefully.

> Arms and the man I sing, the first who came,
> Compelled by fate, an exile out of Troy,
> To Italy and the Lavinian coast,
> Much buffeted on land and on the deep
> By violence of the gods, through that long rage,
> That lasting hate, of Juno's.
>
> (I.1-4)

These first lines tell you that the *Aeneid* has two
major subjects: war and a man. You can already guess
that this man will be a great warrior and that you will
read about many battles. The *Aeneid* also describes
this man's relationship to war: he is both a victim of
war—an "exile," a refugee—and he will also be a con-

queror when he founds his new city in Italy. But this isn't just a war story. It's a story about an individual and how he feels about his life, whom he loves, how he makes his decisions. He is a man "compelled by fate." He doesn't always want to do what he must do; often it isn't even his idea. But the prologue also tells you that this story will have a good ending. The man will reach Italy, and the city he founds will become everlasting Rome. From this we see that the *Aeneid* will also describe the early history of Rome.

NOTE: The role of fate in men's lives is a crucial theme. As you read, ask yourself what that role is. Is fate a force for good or evil? Or is it neutral? Do men have any free choice? Are they responsible for their actions?

One of the most important things the prologue tells you is that the goddess Juno is responsible for much of this man's troubles. Why is she so furious? One reason is that Juno has discovered that the Romans are fated to destroy her favorite city, Carthage. (This actually happened in 146 B.C. during the Third Punic War, about a century before Virgil wrote the *Aeneid*.) The second reason is that she's been nursing a grudge against the Trojans since a Trojan named Paris didn't award her first prize in a beauty contest. The first reason seems a little odd: why is a goddess fighting fate? If fate is inevitable, why fight? Or can Juno win? The second reason is petty. What kind of goddess persecutes a good, honest, and religious man simply because she lost a beauty contest—especially when that man didn't have anything to do with it?

Keep an eye on Juno. She isn't a very admirable character, but she represents an important force in the world Virgil is describing: the power of uncontrolled anger. As you read, see how often rage leads to needless destruction. Later on you'll see that some gods who represent fairness and order, are opposed to Juno. The strange thing is that while they seem much nicer than Juno, they're never as interesting. You might want to think about why Virgil made such a mean character so vivid and real.

After giving you this background, Virgil begins the action. While the Trojans are relaxing in the sunshine, Juno is fuming and wondering whether she has to tolerate these people forever. Even though she knows that they are fated to reach Italy, she's irritated that everyone seems to be ignoring her, while other gods get their way. She decides to cause some trouble. She bribes Aeolus, the god of the winds, to help her sink the Trojan ships. If he'll let the winds out of the cave where he keeps them locked up, she'll give him her prettiest nymph. Of course Aeolus agrees and the winds whip out across the sea.

The sky turns black and winds batter the ships from all directions. Three ships are hurled onto rocks; one is stranded on a shoal; another is sucked into a whirlpool. Men are swimming everywhere, screaming for help. It looks like all is lost as Aeneas makes his first speech, which tells us a lot about his character and about what's on his mind.

> O happy men, thrice happy, four times happy,
> Who had the luck to die, with their fathers
>   watching
> Below the walls of Troy!
>
> (I.94-96)

Aeneas is obviously nostalgic for his lost city of Troy. He misses it so much that he seems to wish he had died there. We also see Aeneas' reverence for his ancestors. (Later on you'll find out that his father had died just before this storm.) Aeneas also respects the old ideal of a hero. He thinks it's better to die fighting for your country than to be lost at sea for no reason. At this point you might be wondering how good a leader Aeneas will be. He literally wants to give up the ship without even trying.

But luckily for the Trojans, Juno is not the only god watching them. Neptune, the god of the sea, notices the uproar in his kingdom and is irritated about it. Unlike Juno, Neptune represents order. He scolds the winds and sends them back to their cave. He drives his flying chariot over the waves and calms them. He rescues the stranded ships. Virgil describes the scene in the first of the famous "epic similes" in the *Aeneid*.

> Sometimes in a great nation, there are riots
> With the rabble out of hand, and firebrands fly
> And cobblestones: whatever they lay their hands
>   on
> Is a weapon for their fury, but should they see
> One man of noble presence, they fall silent
> Obedient dogs, with ears pricked up, and
>   waiting,
> Waiting his word, and he knows how to bring
>   them
> Back to good sense again. So ocean, roaring,
> Subsided into stillness, and the sea-god
> Looked forth upon the waters, and clear
>   weather
> Shone over him as he drove his flying horses.
>   (I.148-156)

In this simile Virgil has described the storm as though it were a civil war, with people fighting in the streets. He shows that a strong leader can calm the people and bring order out of chaos. You'll recall that, when Virgil began the *Aeneid*, the emperor Augustus had finally ended a century of civil strife by his strong leadership. In this way Virgil relates his story to recent events in Rome.

NOTE: An epic simile is a poetic device in which one thing, such as a storm at sea, is compared to another thing, such as a civil war. We won't discuss all the epic similes in the *Aeneid*, but you can have fun trying to spot them. They often begin with "like" or "as" and they usually compare a person or event with something in nature.

Saved from the storm, Aeneas and the remainder of his fleet find themselves near the north coast of Africa and head for the nearest harbor. Even though Aeneas is exhausted, he climbs a mountain, hoping to signal a passing ship. No luck. But suddenly three stags and a herd of deer appear. Quickly he shoots seven with his arrows and carries them back to the Trojan camp. There the men find some wine, still safe in one of the ships, and everyone stretches out on the grass, sipping wine while the meat cooks.

Aeneas gives a little speech, telling his comrades to cheer up, to forget their fear and sadness, and to hope for better days that fate has promised. What he doesn't mention—this is typical of Aeneas—is his own sorrow over his lost comrades and his dread about the future. We begin to see that Aeneas does have leadership qualities: for one, he takes responsibility. But we also see that he hides his true feelings in order to do so.

At this point the scene shifts back to the gods and we are introduced to Jupiter (also called Jove), the king of the gods, and Venus, who is Aeneas' mother.

NOTE: In classical mythology the gods sometimes had children with mortal men and women.
Aeneas is the son of Venus and a mortal man, Anchises. Later on, you'll see that people often call Aeneas
"goddess-born." This means that he is semidivine.
This myth explains why Julius Caesar, who claimed
that he was descended from Aeneas, could proclaim
himself a god while he was emperor. While Augustus
didn't go quite this far, he was revered in Rome as
godlike because he restored peace.

Venus is upset. She reminds Jupiter of his promise
that the Trojans would found Rome and that Rome
would rule the world. Jupiter is perfectly calm and
tells Venus that everything is going just as it should,
according to fate. To calm her he prophesies that
Aeneas will find Italy, win a great war there, and start
his city, Lavinium. (In the *Aeneid*, Italy is sometimes
called Latium or Lavinia. Lavinium and Alba Longa
are the names of the cities that came before the actual
founding of Rome). Three hundred thirty-three years
from this time, Romulus and Remus will build the
walls around the city and call it Rome, after Romulus.

> To these I set no bounds in space or time;
> They shall rule forever . . .
>   And from this great line
> Will come a Trojan, Caesar, to establish
> The limit of his empire at the ocean,
> His glory at the stars, a man called Julius
> Whose name recalls Iulus.
>
>   (I. 278–88)

You can imagine how much the Romans of Virgil's
day enjoyed hearing that they were destined to rule
forever! By making Jupiter predict the future, Virgil

makes the past relevant to present-day Rome. We
understand that this story, which seems to be about
ancient history, will also tell us something about what
kind of people the Romans are and how they got that
way.

NOTE: Iulus is one of the names of Aeneas' son.
(His other name is Ascanius.) By showing the similarity between Iulus' and Julius Caesar's names, Virgil
seems to be supporting Julius Caesar's claim that he
was descended from the original Trojans. Some readers have said that the *Aeneid* is political propaganda
for the emperors Julius and Augustus. In this passage
you can certainly see their point.

Meanwhile Aeneas, who hasn't heard about the
great things that will happen for his people, awakens
the next day and explores the forest to try to deter-
mine what land he is in. A beautiful young girl,
dressed like a huntress, appears and Aeneas immediately suspects she's a goddess. (Virgil tells us that
she's Venus.) She tells Aeneas that he's landed near
Carthage, which is ruled by a woman, Queen Dido.
Dido fled to Carthage after her brother murdered her
husband and she's remained unmarried ever since.

Can you guess what's about to happen? Dido and
Aeneas have much in common. They both had to flee
from home. They're lonely, and they're both the leaders of their people.

Venus wraps Aeneas in a cloud so that he walks
into Carthage without being seen. The city is bustling
and everybody seems happy. Aeneas remarks envi-
ously,

Happy the men whose walls already rise!
                                                    (I. 437)

Dido is building a temple to Juno. (Remember that Carthage is Juno's favorite city.) Its walls are covered with paintings of the Trojan War. Aeneas is amazed and cries at the sight of all his old friends, but it also makes him feel at home. While he's studying each scene, Dido arrives, dressed in gold and followed by her servants. Right behind her, Aeneas sees the comrades he thought had drowned in the storm. Dido kindly assures the Trojans that they are welcome in her kingdom.

At this, Aeneas's cloud melts and he is revealed, looking godlike with the sun shining on his hair and armor. He thanks Dido graciously and greets his lost men.

Dido orders a great feast to celebrate, and things seem to be looking up for the Trojans. But Venus still isn't satisfied. She knows that Carthage is Juno's favorite city and she's afraid that Juno may make Dido turn against Aeneas. So Venus invents a scheme. She has Cupid, the god of love, dress like Ascanius (Aeneas' son) while she puts the real Ascanius to sleep. Cupid's mission is to infect Dido with a "blazing passion" for Aeneas so that Juno won't be able to influence Dido against him.

The scheme works. Dido can't take her eyes off the little boy—or Aeneas, either. It becomes very late but Dido is enjoying herself so much that she won't let anyone go to bed. She begs Aeneas to tell his story—from the beginning. He agrees. In Books II and III we'll hear what he has to say.

NOTE: You are familiar with the pictures of Cupid with his bow and arrow on Valentine's Day cards. That's exactly what Virgil had in mind with this scene. Although we think that love develops inside a person, Dido is "wounded" by love that comes from outside herself. She can't help it. Keep this image of a wound in mind; you'll see it again in Book IV. Note also how Dido's passion is described as a fire. That's also an important image you'll see again. These violent, destructive images suggest that this love affair may not have a happy ending.

BOOK II

Have you ever noticed that, if something really frightening happens, no matter how long ago, you can remember every detail as if it happened yesterday? That's the way Aeneas remembers the last day of Troy before the Greeks destroyed it. Aeneas' story in Book II falls into three basic parts. First, he describes how the Greeks tricked the Trojans into letting them into the city. Second, he describes the desperate final battle to save Troy. Finally, he tells how he escapes from the burning city with his family. An important thing to remember about this Book (and Book III) is that the story is told from Aeneas' point of view. You are about to experience that last dreadful day as though you were there—inside Aeneas' head.

First here is some background. The Trojan War started because Paris, a Trojan, seduced Helen, who was married to a Greek named Menelaus, and took her back to Troy. The Greeks then attacked the Trojans. When Aeneas begins his story, both sides are exhausted. The Greeks have been camped outside the Trojan walls for ten years, unable to get inside. But the Trojans can't drive the Greeks away, either. The result is a stalemate.

Then one morning the Trojans look over their walls
and the Greeks are gone! In their place they've left a
giant wooden horse. The Trojans throw open the
gates and rush out, wild with joy.

In fact, the Greeks aren't gone at all. Some of them
are hiding on a nearby island, Tenedos, where
they've hidden their ships. The rest are hiding in the
hollow belly of the huge horse—waiting.

An ironic twist in the story is that one of the Trojans, Laocoön, warns that the Greeks are probably
hiding inside the horse, but no one listens to him.
Instead, the Trojans believe the story of a Greek
named Sinon, who deliberately allowed himself to be
"captured." Sinon tells them that if they destroy the
horse, the gods will be furious and Troy will be
destroyed. If, on the other hand, they bring the horse
inside the city walls, Troy will conquer the Greeks.

> We believed him, we
> Whom neither Diomede nor great Achilles
> Had taken, nor ten years, nor that armada,
> A thousand ships of war. But Sinon did it
> By perjury and guile.
>
> (II. 195–98)

Aeneas points out here that lies and tricks can do
what the greatest Greek warriors and ten years of war
could not. Deceit and treachery are important themes
in Book II.

Another thing that convinces the Trojans to bring
the horse into the city is that Laocoön, who warned
them not to do this, is strangled horribly by two giant
snakes that come rushing over the sea from Tenedos
(just as the Greeks will attack later on). The snakes'
eyes are burning with blood and fire as they choke
Laocoön. The Trojans correctly decide that Laocoön is

being punished, but they don't realize that he's being punished for telling the truth about the horse. The gods side with the Greeks, and they don't want anyone to save Troy.

NOTE: Snakes are an important image in this Book. They symbolize evil and deception and whenever they appear, destruction is not far behind. Fire is also a symbol of destruction. As you read Book II you will see many images of snakes and fire.

The Trojans put the horse on wheels and slowly drag it inside the city. As they do, they can hear clanking inside it. What's the matter with the Trojans? Are they stupid? Perhaps. Or did the gods blind them to the obvious danger? But the gods could have destroyed Troy if they had wanted to. Why do they make the Trojans cooperate in their own downfall? Perhaps Virgil is saying that the division between human beings and the gods and fate is not so simple. Perhaps what happens to you depends, in part, on the kind of person you are. The Trojans were tired of war and wanted to believe it was over. Perhaps their wishful thinking brought their downfall. Have you ever taken a big risk that you knew wasn't a good idea, but you just kept your fingers crossed and hoped that it would work out anyway?

The Trojans celebrate their false victory with a wild festival that night, and then they all collapse into their beds in a drunken sleep. In the dark and quiet of night, the Greeks sail back. Sinon undoes the bolts on the belly of the horse and the Greeks pour out. They start to murder everyone in their path.

While Aeneas sleeps, Hector appears to him in a dream. (Hector was a great Trojan warrior who was killed by the Greek Achilles.)

Alas, O goddess-born! Take flight,
Escape these flames! The enemy has the walls,
Troy topples from her lofty height; enough
Has been paid out to Priam and to country.
(II. 289–91)

Hector then tells Aeneas to take the household
gods of Troy (small figures that symbolized the gods
that protected a home), and to build a new city after a
long sea voyage. Hector's speech is more than just a
warning. This is the first time that Aeneas hears of his
destiny to lead his people to a new city. Hector also
tells Aeneas that he no longer has a soldier's duty to
fight for his king, Priam, or his country. Why is this
important? Aeneas might think it was cowardly to run
away, but Hector is trying to tell him that it's the only
sensible thing to do.

Aeneas jumps out of bed and sees that the Greeks
are already swarming all over Troy and that most of
the buildings are in flames. But Aeneas doesn't seem
to have understood Hector's message very well.
Instead of fleeing, he stays and fights, although even
he realizes there's no hope. Why does he risk his life?
One reason is that he simply gets carried away when
he sees his city being destroyed. But there may be
more to it. Sometimes it's easier to keep fighting for a
lost cause than to admit defeat and start something
completely new. As we'll see later on, Aeneas isn't
very eager to start a new life somewhere else.

In the second part of Book II, Aeneas and his men
struggle in vain to save Troy. The battle is fought at
night, so the only light comes from the burning ruins
of Troy. In this flickering light no one is sure who
anyone is. The Trojans kill some Greeks and take their
armor. Disguised like this, they score some victories—until their fellow Trojans, trying to defend the

walls, also mistake them for Greeks and start to hurl weapons at their heads.

Finally, Aeneas manages to reach King Priam's castle. The battle for the ramparts rages here, and Aeneas sees the most horrible scene of all. A Greek warrior, Pyrrhus, who is "sleek as a serpent," murders Priam's son right before his father's eyes. Then he kills the old and feeble king on the altar dedicated to the gods. In this sad scene, we see the horror of uncontrolled rage and the total collapse of the old heroic ideals of fair play and respect for one's enemies. The serpents, like Pyrrhus, are winning this war.

Suddenly Aeneas spots Helen hiding. He's about to kill her, in revenge for the war she helped to cause, when Venus bursts upon the scene and stops him. She reminds him to take care of his family instead of seeking pointless revenge. Then she gives Aeneas a moment of divine vision, so that he can see that it's not only the Greeks who are destroying Troy. He sees that the gods, themselves, are smashing the walls. At last Aeneas understands that there's no point in fighting anymore, and he hurries off to find his family. Here we see that with Venus' help, Aeneas helps to save lives, instead of being purely destructive like Pyrrhus.

When Aeneas reaches his father's house, he runs into still another roadblock to leaving. His father, Anchises, won't budge. He's old and tired; he doesn't see the point in leaving. Just then a flame appears over the head of Aeneas' son, Iulus. Before they can recover from their surprise, a comet streaks across the sky. After these signs, even Anchises believes that the gods are with Aeneas and his son and that they have a special mission.

They leave. Aeneas carries his old father on his back and holds his little son by the hand. His wife, Creusa, follows. Aeneas has literally shouldered the burden of saving his family and their future. Somehow, in the dark and confusion, Creusa becomes separated from them. Aeneas is frantic and returns to the burning city trying to find her. Suddenly her ghost appears and tells him to stop looking. She explains that he has a great journey ahead and that he will find a happier land in the west. She also tells him that he will find a new wife of royal blood.

Aeneas is miserable with grief and reaches out for her shadow but it flits aways. Why is Creusa left behind and why does she tell Aeneas to go on? Her death symbolizes the end of his old life in Troy. Aeneas must leave her and start a new life. An important theme in the *Aeneid* is that Aeneas must suffer many deep personal losses in order to fulfill his destiny. He doesn't accept those losses easily. He reaches out for Creusa three times, and three times she fades away, before he accepts the fact that she is dead.

Finally, he rejoins his father and son. They have been joined by a band of other Trojans who have escaped the city. Together they climb into the hills.

BOOK III

Aeneas has just finished his sad story about the fall of Troy. He pauses for breath and perhaps sips some wine. Dido wipes the tears from her eyes. The Trojans gaze at the flickering torches, remembering the past.

Then Aeneas begins to talk again. In Book III he describes how he and the Trojans have been searching for a place to live, for the seven years since the day

Troy fell to the storm that blew them to Carthage. Have you ever had a bad dream in which you were trying to reach a place or to find something, and you just couldn't? That's the mood of Book III. The Trojans have a vague idea that they are fated to find a new home somewhere in the west. The gods give them a few clues about where the place is, but the clues aren't very clear and the Trojans don't understand them. So they keep landing their ships and trying to settle down, but something always goes wrong and they have to pack up again.

Troy was located on the coast of present-day Turkey. If you look at the map on page 45, you'll see that at first the Trojans keep trying to make a new home very close to their old one. They move closer and closer to Italy only after they are driven from more familiar spots by evil omens, plagues, or Harpies. Their first stop is Thrace, but the ghost of a Trojan murdered by the Thracians warns them that it's not safe. They then reach the island of Delos where there was a shrine to Apollo, who could foretell the future. Aeneas prays before the temple and Apollo answers:

> The land which brought you forth,
> Men of endurance, will receive you home.
> Seek out your ancient mother.
>
> (III. 93–95)

The Trojans are delighted with this advice, but they can't figure out what place Apollo refers to. Then Anchises decides that the god means Crete because one of the Trojans' early ancestors had come from Crete. The Trojans leap in their boats and one races against the other to get to Crete first. However, within a year they realize that Crete isn't correct, either. They are stricken with plagues and drought.

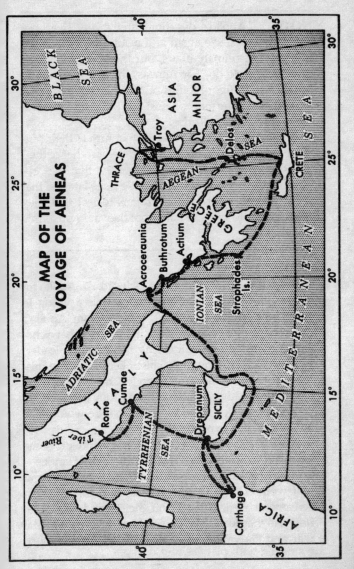

MAP OF THE
VOYAGE OF AENEAS

NOTE: Apollo's directions aren't very clear, are
they? As you'll see again and again, the gods often
intervene in human affairs, but they rarely tell men
exactly what to do. For Aeneas, the result is that he
must learn to figure things out for himself and must
struggle when he makes a mistake. In the end this will
make him a better leader.

When Apollo tells the Trojans to return to their "ancient mother" he means Italy, because another of their
ancestors came from Italy. This means that the Trojans originally came from Italy. We'll see later on that
it's very important for the Trojans to feel that they
have a right to settle in Italy, that they are not simply
invaders.

Anchises wants to return to Delos to ask Apollo for
better directions. However, Aeneas has a vision in
which the Trojan household gods explain Apollo's
meaning to him. You see here that the gods have cho-
sen Aeneas, not Anchises, as the Trojans' leader.
However, even though Anchises keeps making mistakes such as the decision to go to Crete, Aeneas still
asks him for advice. Aeneas hasn't fully accepted his
role as leader yet. Soon we'll see that he won't have
any choice but to accept it.

After a storm at sea, the Trojans land on some
islands (the Strophades) that belong to the Harpies—
horrible, foul-smelling creatures that are half bird and
half woman. The Harpies attack, and one of them
screams at Aeneas to get off their island and go to
Italy. As they leave, she curses them, telling them that
war and starvation await them there. They'll be so

hungry she says, that they'll eat their tables. It's not an inviting prospect, is it?

The Trojans' next important stop is a very strange place: Buthrotum. You can imagine what Disneyland is like. That's what Buthrotum must have seemed like to the Trojans. Built by two exiles from Troy, Helenus and Andromache, Buthrotum resembled a miniature Troy with a small river like the Xanthus, and copies of the Trojan walls and city gates.

Andromache is the widow of Hector, the great Trojan warrior killed by Achilles. When Aeneas first sees her, she is weeping outside an empty tomb that she's built in Hector's memory. Although she's married again and many years have passed, she's still mourning. As she and Aeneas reminisce about the old days she keeps bursting into tears.

Helenus and Andromache welcome the Trojans warmly. They can remain at Buthrotum forever if they want to. In many ways it seems right because it's so much like Troy. But Aeneas is eager to move on. Why? It's important to see that this episode is different from the others we've seen in this Book. This is the first place that Aeneas leaves without being forced to. For the first time, he seems to be accepting his fate. He realizes that Helenus and Andromache are rooted in the past—as nice as that may be—but that he must start a new life.

Before he leaves, Aeneas gets detailed directions from Helenus about where to go and what dangers to avoid. Helenus explains that they must reach the west coast of Italy, and that they should get there by sailing all the way around Sicily to avoid Scylla and Charybdis, who guard the narrow strait between Sicily and Italy. (Scylla was a six-headed monster that devoured ships. Charybdis was a whirlpool that sucked in ships.)

The Trojans reach Sicily and land near Mount Etna—a place inhabited by Cyclopes, who are horrible, gory, one-eyed monsters that eat men. The Trojans spend a terrible night underneath the mountain, which is a volcano and belches smoke and lava. In the morning a ragged, starving man, a Greek left behind by Ulysses, runs out of the woods and warns them to flee. They escape just as one of the Cyclopes, who was blinded by Ulysses, comes roaring and stomping down to the beach to wash his oozing eye.

NOTE: In this incident, Virgil is deliberately reminding us of one of the episodes in the Greek epic, the *Odyssey*, by Homer. In that epic the hero, Ulysses, spends many years searching for his home, just as Aeneas does. Having Aeneas stop in one of the places where Ulysses stopped is one of the ways in which Virgil suggests that his hero is as great as the famous Ulysses.

At last the Trojans manage to sail to the west coast of Sicily and land at Drepanum. Now they are very close to their destination. But then something terrible happens: Anchises dies. Aeneas is heartbroken.

> All the storms and perils,
> All of the weariness endured, seemed nothing
> Compared with this disaster.
>
> *(III. 708–11)*

On this sad note Aeneas ends his story to Dido. He's a lonely and worn-out man. After all he's been through since the fall of Troy, he feels that the worst is the loss of his father, the person he consulted for advice. Just as he was about to reach Italy, this happened. He remembers carrying his father out of burning Troy and wonders what the point of it was. Now he must make all his decisions alone.

NOTE: Do you see how the story has come full circle? In Book I, you read how Juno created a storm just as the Trojans were leaving Sicily in order to prevent them from reaching Italy. Instead, they were blown to Carthage, and Aeneas tells his story to Dido. In a sense we're back to the point we started from. In the next Book we'll see what happens to Aeneas and Dido.

BOOK IV

Have you ever had a crush on someone? Who knows why it happens, but one day you meet someone special and the next thing you know you're lying awake at night thinking about him or her. Everything else begins to bore you. You can only think of one person. That's how Dido feels when Aeneas finishes his story.

> Soft fire consumes the marrow-bones, the silent
> Wound grows, deep in the heart.
> Unhappy Dido burns, and wanders, burning,
> All up and down the city, the way a deer
> With a hunter's careless arrow in her flank
> Ranges the uplands, with the shaft still clinging
> To the hurt side.
>
> (IV. 66–73)

Remember how Dido's love was described as a "wound" in Book I? Here's the same imagery again. Note how Virgil also uses the image of fire. In Book II,

Virgil used fire imagery to describe the destructive power of anger and war. Here he uses it to describe how dangerous passionate love can be.

NOTE: The description of Dido as a wounded deer is another epic simile. The hunter was careless; he didn't mean to shoot the deer. Keep this image in mind as you try to decide whether or not Aeneas is responsible for what happens to Dido. Do you think Virgil is hinting that Dido is a victim of Aeneas? Of the gods? Or maybe even of herself?

After her husband was murdered, Dido had vowed never to marry again. Now her sister, Anna, tells her that she's been a widow long enough and that it would be good for Carthage if she married Aeneas. Anna means well, but she's encouraging Dido to make a fatal mistake.

Juno sees what's happening to her favorite queen and quickly devises a plan to help Dido get what she wants—and also to keep the Trojans from reaching Italy. She sweetly suggests to Venus that they should make Aeneas and Dido marry. Venus agrees with this because she knows that Aeneas is fated to reach Italy and that the marriage can never last.

Why doesn't Juno realize this, too? The answer must be that Juno is irrational. That's one of the reasons she's so destructive. She's always fighting the inevitable. The result can only be trouble—even for people she likes, such as Dido.

The next morning the two goddesses carry out their scheme. Aeneas and Dido go hunting with a great crowd of Trojans and Carthaginians. They both look wonderful. Suddenly a huge storm whips up and everyone dashes for shelter. (Remember that storms

are one of Juno's favorite tricks.) Aeneas and Dido
find themselves in the same cave—alone. What happens next? Virgil is too refined to tell us, but he does
say that Dido decides to call this "natural" ceremony a
marriage. She's so in love with Aeneas that she forgets her reputation and her position as queen. It's not
long before rumors of what's happened spread all
over Carthage. Aeneas and Dido spend a wonderful
year together but, in the meantime, all the work in
Carthage grinds to a halt and the Trojans sit, waiting
for directions from their leader.

Finally, Jupiter gets angry at Aeneas for spending
so much time in Carthage and avoiding his destiny.
He sends Mercury, the messenger of the gods, with a
message for Aeneas to get going.

> If your own fame and fortune count as nothing,
> Think of Ascanius at least, whose kingdom
> In Italy, whose Roman land, are waiting.
> (IV. 273–75)

Aeneas is horrified that he has forgotten his duty to
his country and to his son, and he decides to leave for
Italy as soon as possible. But he has one big problem:
how will he break the news to Dido? He can't think of
anything, so he delays, hoping that the right moment
will arise. In the meantime he orders his men to ready
the fleet.

Dido sees all the hustle and bustle in the harbor and
guesses the truth. She's had no warning and becomes
hysterical. Before Aeneas has a chance to explain himself, she accuses him of betraying her and trying to
sneak away like a coward.

Aeneas has a hard time deciding what to say. When
he finally says something, it's just the opposite of
Dido's passionate outburst. He says that they weren't
really married, and he explains that he must leave

because the fates tell him to. While he says that he has great respect for Dido, he never says that he loves her or wishes he could stay.

Dido watches him out of the corner of her eyes, hoping for some hint of emotion. When she sees nothing, she goes into a frenzy of despair and decides to kill herself. Her servants carry her away.

Virgil tells us that Aeneas really is very upset, but that as leader of his people he feels he must do what fate and the gods tell him to do. His sense of duty is stronger than his love. He swallows his feelings and deals with Dido in a purely rational way. Some readers think this is a cold and heartless way to behave. Others believe Aeneas' self-control is heroic. Which interpretation seems right to you?

Imagine that you're going steady with someone a year or two younger than you are. You are accepted into college far away from home. What do you do? Stay at home with the person you love or go away to college? If you go, how do you break the news?

Even if you decide that Aeneas did the right thing by leaving, that doesn't mean that he was right to get involved with Dido in the first place. Because he knew he had to reach Italy, his actions were rather careless. (Remember that careless hunter at the beginning of this book?) You begin to see that Carthage, where Aeneas became involved with Dido, is a mistake just like all the places in Book III where the Trojans tried to settle.

What about Dido? We've already seen that in many ways she's not to blame for what happened. Venus made her fall in love. And she is also a victim of Aeneas' fate that he must reach Italy. On the other hand, some readers feel that Dido contributes to her own tragedy because she forgets her responsibility as queen. She recklessly "marries" Aeneas without considering her reputation and the effect the marriage will have on her authority. While she is distracted by love, all the work in Carthage comes to a halt.

After Dido is carried out, Aeneas returns to his ships. Dido, watching from her window, bursts into tears and sends Anna to beg Aeneas to stay just a little while longer for Dido's sake. But Aeneas has made up his mind and nothing can change it. In one of Virgil's most beautiful epic similes, Virgil compares Aeneas to a giant oak tree that no wind or storm can knock down.

Aeneas has changed since the earlier books where he was never sure what to do or where to go. This simile tells us what Virgil thinks a good Roman leader should be. Once he decides what's right, he has to be able to stick to his decision, regardless of how people try to dissuade him.

Dido builds a funeral pyre, decorates it with garlands, and drapes it with Aeneas' armor and sword. All night she tosses and turns with grief, regret, and guilt. At dawn, she looks out her window and discovers that the Trojans have already left!

She curses Aeneas and vows that the Carthaginian people will always hate the Romans, and that a great man will arise to avenge the wrong Aeneas did to her. (Dido's curse comes true. Romans of Virgil's time would understand that this curse referred to the Punic Wars between Carthage and Rome and that the great avenger would be Hannibal, a Carthaginian general who almost conquered Rome.) Then, trembling in frenzy, Dido climbs the funeral pyre, throws herself on Aeneas' sword, and dies.

Dido is a very real and convincing character. You feel sorry for what happens to her. If this Book of the *Aeneid* is your favorite, you'll be happy to know that many other people agree with you. This realistic depiction of a woman and a passionate love affair is the first of its kind in Western literature. It's been imitated, discussed, and argued about ever since it was written.

NOTE: As you think about how the *Aeneid* relates to Rome at the time Virgil was writing, you should know that Dido may represent Cleopatra. Like Dido, Cleopatra was the queen of an African country. Like Dido, she was loved by one of the great Romans leaders, Marc Antony. Antony and Cleopatra wanted to combine Egypt and the Roman Empire and rule together, but Augustus defeated them at Actium in 31 B.C. and Cleopatra committed suicide. While Aeneas is "wasting time" in Carthage, Romans of the day probably would have compared him to Marc Antony. After Aeneas leaves, he must have seemed more like the cool, clear-headed Augustus, whom Cleopatra had once tried to seduce.

BOOK V

Book V gives you a break from the tragedy and difficult moral questions of Book IV. The Trojans return to Drepanum, the place in Sicily where Aeneas' father Anchises had died. When they arrive, the king of Sicily, Acestes, is already on the beach to welcome them with wine and food. Aeneas pays his respects at his father's tomb, and he tells his people that it is exactly a year since Anchises died. Instead of mourning anymore, he suggests that they honor the anniversary by holding great athletic contests, known as funeral games.

NOTE: The Romans, like the Greeks before them (who gave us the model for the Olympic Games), took athletic competition very seriously. Games were one way to practice skills needed in war, and they were often part of the rituals used to honor the dead. The competitions took people's minds off their worries and affirmed their sense of strength and well-being. Games were often part of religious ceremonies, as well. Augustus included them in religious rites in Rome, as part of his program to keep the youth of Rome fit both morally and physically.

In Book V we see five different events. The first is a boat race. Virgil's description of the race is exciting and funny—quite different from the tone we've been reading so far. The crews are straining at the oars; the crowd on shore is cheering wildly. Each boat must sail out to sea, swing around a huge rock, and return to shore. There are four boats and four captains. Gyas' boat takes the lead, but its pilot is too cautious and swings around the rock too widely, giving Cloanthus' boat a chance to get ahead. Gyas is so irritated by this that he throws his pilot overboard. The crowd on shore is hysterical as the poor man climbs onto the rock dripping wet. Sergestus' boat swings too close to the rock and breaks all its oars. But Menestheus makes it safely and begins to gain on Cloanthus. The crew is straining every muscle and they almost overtake Cloanthus but, at the last moment, Cloanthus prays to the gods for help. Then the sea nymphs push his boat over the water faster than Menestheus' men can row.

It's an exciting race and it's fun to read, but it has a hidden moral lesson, too. It's not good to be too cautious, like Gyas' pilot, or too reckless, like Sergestus. The winner chooses a middle course. But winning also depends on the gods' help. The man who prays wins. Here we see three basic virtues that the Romans of Virgil's day certainly respected: skill, moderation, and piety.

Aeneas gives the first prize to Cloanthus, but also gives an award to each of the other captains. He does the same thing in each of the other contests too, showing that he knows how to keep everybody in good humor.

Each of the contests that follow also illustrates a virtue or moral. For example, the footraces show the power of friendship. The young and swift Trojan men line up on the starting line and dash across a grassy field. Among them are Nisus and Euryalus, who are best friends. Nisus is in the lead and is about to win when he slips and falls. Realizing that he no longer has a chance, he cleverly trips the racer right behind him so that Euryalus wins.

In the boxing arena, an old Sicilian fights a young, overconfident Trojan and shows that skill and experience can be more powerful than youthful strength and quickness. In the archery contest, the Trojans' respect for the gods is shown. King Acestes wins first prize, not because he hits the target, but because his arrow bursts into flame as it flies—clearly an act of the gods. In the final event, the Trojan boys, led by Aeneas' son Ascanius, show their skills as riders in mock war games. Virgil tells us that the Roman boys still practiced these exercises in his day.

While the men are having all this fun, however, the women are moping on the beach by the ships. They're sick and tired of traveling. As you might expect, Juno sees her chance to cause more trouble. She sends a goddess named Iris, disguised as one of the women, to urge them to burn the fleet. Iris throws the first torch and the women go into a frenzy. Each grabs a torch and hurls it. The ships burst into flames. (Here is the imagery of fire and destruction again.)

When Aeneas discovers what's happened, he despairs. He prays to Jupiter for help. Sure enough, the heavens open up and a huge downpour puts out the fires. Only four ships are beyond repair.

But the women's irritability and weariness have given Aeneas new doubts. He can see their point. An old and wise sailor suggests that they leave the women, as well as the old and sick, behind in Sicily under the protection of King Acestes. Aeneas can't decide what to do until the spirit of his dead father appears to him and tells him that the sailor's advice is good. Anchises also tells Aeneas that when he gets to Italy, he must descend to the underworld and visit Anchises. Then Anchises will be able to show Aeneas what the future holds for his people.

Note that leaving the women behind changes the character of the Trojan group. The men who will land in Italy are warriors. Instead of a band of homeless exiles, with their wives and children, this group looks much more like an invading army. You'll see that this becomes an important asset in the second half of the *Aeneid*.

Venus wants to make sure that this time the Trojans really get to Italy. So she asks Neptune to give them calm sailing. He agrees but demands one life in return. The unlucky victim is Palinurus, Aeneas' faithful pilot. In the middle of the calm night, as the ships glide gently over the water, the god of sleep makes Palinurus fall asleep and then throws him overboard. Aeneas wakes up to discover the ship drifting aimlessly and his pilot gone. Mourning for his lost comrade, he guides the boat himself to Italy.

NOTE: In this scene you see a good example of a theme we find hard to understand today—the belief that the gods demand the sacrifice of innocent victims. The Trojans—and the Romans of Virgil's day—often sacrificed animals. Sometimes the gods demanded people as well. In a way, wasn't Dido sacrificed to the gods' larger plans?

But you can also think about this incident in another way. You don't have to believe in the gods to imagine how this accident could have happened naturally. Palinurus is sitting up all night with no one to talk to. The ship is rocking gently. It's not hard to see why he falls asleep; anyone might. You might begin to suspect that the gods can be seen as forces or tendencies that are part of every person. Thus, the god of sleep isn't outside Palinurus; it's part of him.

BOOK VI

Have you ever had an experience that changed you, changed the kind of person you were? Sometimes, something very sad or shocking can do that to you. Sometimes, it can be something beautiful and simple like the first really warm day in spring. Whatever does it, one day you wake up and have a whole new outlook on life. You understand something about yourself or about what you want out of life that you never realized before.

That's what happens to Aeneas in Book VI. Almost every great religion or culture—from Christianity to Buddhism—has a story about death and rebirth. Virgil uses the same theme in Book VI to show how the old uncertain Aeneas, the Aeneas whose heart is stuck in ruined Troy, dies and comes back a new, determined Aeneas, committed to Italy and its future.

How does Virgil do this? He has Aeneas journey to the underworld, the place in Greek and Roman mythology where dead souls or "shades" live. Aeneas doesn't actually die. His trip allows him to see what it would be like to be dead without really dying. In the process, he meets many peole who lived both good and bad lives and from this he learns what really counts. This new insight makes his old, regretful self "die." What's more, in the underworld his father shows him the future in a parade of great Romans who will be born. Aeneas is inspired. For the first time, he has hope in the future. He decides that his fate is worth pursuing, instead of avoiding. He starts to do things because he wants to, not just because he has to.

As you can see, Book VI is important because it describes a major turning point for Aeneas. Aeneas' travels so far can be interpreted as a symbolic journey of a person in search of a new identity. In Book VI, Aeneas finally finds out who he is—the person who will make the Roman Empire possible. Let's see how that happens.

As Book VI opens, the Trojans have just landed at Cumae on the west coast of Italy near present-day Naples. The men are ecstatic, but Aeneas, who always does his duty first, goes looking for the Sibyl. (Remember that in Book III Helenus told him to go see the Sibyl as soon as he got to Italy.) The Sibyl, a priestess of Apollo, can foresee the future. When Aeneas asks his fortune, the Sibyl reels and spins and all the doors of Apollo's temple fly open. She goes into a trance and Apollo speaks through her.

> War, I see,
> Terrible war, and the river Tiber foaming
> With streams of blood. There will be another
>   Xanthus,
> Another Simois, and Greek encampment,
> Even another Achilles, born in Latium,
> Himself a goddess' son.
>
> *(VI. 86–90)*

Poor Aeneas! He's come all this way to find out that he's headed for another war, a war that will be a replay of the Trojan War. (Xanthus and Simois were rivers near Troy.) He will even have to face another warrior as fierce as Achilles.

NOTE: It's important to keep this prediction in mind as you read Books VII–XII of the *Aeneid*. The war in Italy will parallel the Trojan War in many ways except that, as you already know, the Trojans will win. Why do the Trojans win this time? Is it because of fate or the gods, because their cause is just, or because the Trojans have changed since Troy? You'll have to wait and see. But in the meantime, note how this prediction fits in with the theme of death and rebirth. Troy died, but in a way it's going to live again. The Trojans are going to get a second chance.

If Aeneas is upset he doesn't show it, but he quickly changes the subject to his second reason for coming to the Sibyl. He needs her help to reach the underworld to visit his father, as Anchises told him to do in Book V.

The Sibyl tells Aeneas that in order to come back alive he must first bury one of his men, who has died without his knowing it, and second that he must find a golden bough of a tree. Aeneas finds the man and goes into the forest to cut wood for his funeral pyre. He's wondering how he can possibly find a golden bough, when Venus sends two white doves who show him where it is. (The golden bough is a famous symbol for resurrection. *The Golden Bough* is the title of a well-known book by James Frazer, which describes many different myths on this theme.)

Now, Aeneas and the Sibyl are ready for their journey. Aeneas follows her into a huge dark cave that the ancient Romans believed was the mouth of the underworld. (There really is a huge cave near Cumae.) Aeneas can hardly see where he's going. Strange shapes flit by him as he descends. He draws his sword, but the Sibyl warns him that they are only phantoms.

They reach the underworld river, Acheron, where a sour old man named Charon ferries across dead souls. He will only take souls who have been buried. Here Aeneas sees his former pilot, Palinurus, who tells him that his body is lying on the coast of Italy—unburied. He begs Aeneas to help him cross the river, but the Sibyl interrupts and hurries Aeneas on. We see the finality of death. Palinurus' fate is sealed and Aeneas can no longer help him, even though Aeneas really wants to.

They cross the Acheron and come to the Fields of Mourning, where souls who were ruined by love stay. Aeneas has a shock when he sees Dido here. He reaches out to her and tries to talk to her and offer some consolation, but Dido turns her back and walks away. Remember, in Book IV, how Aeneas couldn't or wouldn't say anything to make Dido feel any better? This time the tables are turned and it is Dido who can't or won't say anything to make Aeneas feel any better. Here, again, we see how death ends everything. Aeneas would like to try to make things a little better between them. But Dido can't change. She's fixed in her sorrow and anger.

They pass other sad characters and avoid the place where people who led wicked lives are tortured forever. Included here are people who caused civil wars. Remember how much Virgil hated the civil wars in Rome before Augustus put an end to them? He gets his revenge by putting all those people in hell.

Finally they pass through some gates and leave the sad and dark part of the underworld behind. Aeneas sees a beautiful world of green fields, sunlight, and flowers. This is Elysium, the part of the underworld for those who have led good and productive lives. Anchises is here. Aeneas bursts into tears and tries to hug his father, but Anchises is only a shade and he flutters away. Aeneas must be content to talk.

Anchises points into the distance and shows Aeneas a group of shades who are ready to return to life. Aeneas can't believe that anyone would deliberately go back to the upper world with all its hardships. But Anchises explains that souls are purified in the underworld for 1000 years and then they drink the waters of forgetfulness so that they can return to life fresh and pure.

NOTE: Doesn't this sound a lot like reincarnation? This idea has been around a long time in many different cultures. Virgil gives us his own brand here, combining ideas from Plato, the Stoics, and other Greek philosophers. Note the parallel to what is going to happen to Aeneas. His short journey into the underworld is going to renew him, give him fresh strength, and make him forget his old Trojan life.

Finally Anchises shows Aeneas the parade of great Romans who will be born in the future. First, he points out the long line of early kings of Alba Longa (the city that Aeneas' son, Ascanius, will build after Aeneas dies). Then he points out Romulus, the legendary founder of Rome itself. Next to Romulus is Augustus, the great rebuilder of Rome after the civil wars. (Note that by putting Augustus right next to Romulus, Virgil seems to be suggesting that Augustus is as great as the founder of Rome.) On the other side of the field, Anchises points to the great leaders of the Roman Republic before Augustus and the great generals, including Julius Caesar and Pompey.

Finally Anchises tells Aeneas that the Romans' great gift will be for ruling.

> To rule the people under law, to establish
> The way of peace, to battle down the haughty,
> To spare the meek. Our fine arts, these, forever.
> *(VI. 852-54)*

Needless to say, Aeneas is inspired by this vision of the future and he returns to the upper world. There are two gates to leave by. One is only for real shades. The other is for false dreams. Aeneas leaves by the gate for false dreams.

What do you make of this exit? Does Aeneas leave by the gate for dreams just because he's not really dead? Or is Virgil telling us something about this vision of Rome's future? Is it just a dream? Will it be true or false depending on what Aeneas does with it? Virgil may be reminding us that though certain things are fated, they still depend on human effort to make them happen.

NOTE: This is a good example of how Virgil art-
fully blends the past, present, and future into his
poem. By having Anchises predict the future, Virgil
gives his readers a short course in Roman history
down to the day he was writing. You can also see how
much this description would have flattered Augustus.
In having Anchises tell Aeneas that the Romans' gift
will be for ruling, Virgil is confirming Augustus'—
and the Roman people's—belief that their empire
would last forever.

At this point, the first half of the *Aeneid* ends. From
now on Aeneas will stay in Italy. What do the first six
books all have in common? They each describe a kind
of journey. Some of the journeys are actual geograph-
ical trips, particularly Books I, III, and V. Others are
more abstract psychological or emotional journeys.
For example, in Book II Aeneas has to leave home and
in the process he loses a clear sense of who he is and
what he's supposed to do. In Book IV, Aeneas takes a
side-trip into his emotions with Dido, only to discover
that that's not what the gods have planned for him. In
Book VI, he takes a trip into the future in the underworld and discovers his new identity and purpose as
a Roman.

BOOK VII

After Aeneas returns from the underworld, he and
his men sail a little way up the coast of Italy until they
get to the mouth of the Tiber (the river that Rome is
built along). The banks of the river are grassy and
cool, and they settle down to eat a frugal meal of wild
fruit, which they put on "tables" of hardtack—
unleavened bread, made in large wafers. They are so

hungry they break the hardtack and eat it too, and Aeneas realizes that this must be the place they were destined to stay. (Remember that the Harpy predicted they would eat their tables in Book III?)

The place where they've landed is Latium, and its king is an old man named Latinus. (The native people are called Latins.) Aeneas sends his best men to bring gifts to Latinus and to make offerings of peace. They explain that they are Trojans and their leader is Aeneas, and they tell how fate has brought them to Latium. All they ask is a little land and freedom to breathe the air and drink the water.

Now old Latinus had an only daughter, Lavinia. Long before the Trojans arrived, the king had been receiving omens that his daughter was destined to marry a foreigner and that she, together with the foreigner, would start a new race that was destined to rule the world. Meanwhile, however, a young warrior, Turnus, had fallen in love with Lavinia and wanted to marry her. Latinus' wife, Amata, particularly liked this young man, but Latinus kept putting off the wedding because of the omens that Lavinia was supposed to marry a stranger.

When the Trojans arrive and tell about their leader Aeneas, a light bulb goes on in Latinus' head. He suspects that Aeneas is the man his daughter is destined to marry. So, he welcomes the Trojans heartily and offers them land and gifts. To the Trojans' amazement he even gives them a message for Aeneas: Aeneas can marry his daughter. Quite a welcome!

NOTE: A marriage between a Trojan man and a woman of a different country has caused a lot of trouble before. Remember how Paris started the Trojan

War by taking Helen away from her Greek husband?
Here Aeneas may take Lavinia away from her Latin
fiancé, Turnus. This is one of the ways in which the
war in Italy will repeat the Trojan War. But there is a
crucial difference between the two situations. Paris
seduced a married woman, but so far Aeneas hasn't
done anything wrong. In fact, he hasn't even met
her!

But nothing ever goes smoothly for the Trojans.
Juno, cruising through the clouds, spots the Trojans
in Latium. The fact that her plot to keep them in Carthage completely fell through only makes her more
incensed at Aeneas. She realizes that she cannot
change fate, but she can delay it with more trouble.

> If I cannot
> Bend Heaven, I can raise Hell. . . .
>   Lavinia, Latium,
> Will come to him in time. It is permitted
> To keep that time far off. It is permitted
> To strike their people down. It will cost them
>   something.
>   (VII. 310-17)

You've seen Juno behave exactly like this before—
at the beginning of Book I when she saw the Trojans
leaving Sicily. Then she whipped up a storm, using
the forces of nature against them. This time she tries
something new. She asks an evil creature from the
underworld, a Fury named Allecto, to plant the seeds
of war in the hearts of men. Note that in Book I Neptune calmed Juno's storm and the Trojans landed
peacefully in Carthage. But no god will stop this war.
Do you think that Virgil may be suggesting that once
fear and anger enter men's hearts only men can stop
it?

Allecto is a horrible, savage creature who loves nothing better than war. She represents uncontrolled rage—like Juno, only more so. Allecto uses three victims to start war. First she infects Amata, Latinus' wife, with poisonous snakes. At first Amata is reasonable. She goes to her husband, crying and asking why their daughter must be married to a foreigner. But when she sees that Latinus won't change his mind, she goes into a wild frenzy, tearing around the streets of the city with her hair and clothes undone. She tries to hide Lavinia in the woods. When the other women see Amata's frenzy, they too get carried away and begin to rush through the city, crying for war against the Trojans.

Next Allecto goes to Turnus, the warrior, while he's sleeping and tells him that his kingdom and bride are about to be given away to the Trojans. At first Turnus replies calmly and tells Allecto to mind her own business. At this she flies into a rage and lights his body with a torch. He starts from sleep, his body on fire for war, infected with Allecto's wrath. (Once again we see fire as a symbol of uncontrollable passion and destruction.)

NOTE: Do you see the similarity between what Allecto does to Turnus and what Cupid did to Dido? Neither person was unreasonable to begin with, but each is infected with blazing passions for love (Dido) or war (Turnus) that rage out of control. We have also seen how the gods can represent forces that are part of people's personalities, even if they didn't let them show. For example, is it possible that the lust for war, which is part of Turnus' personality as a warrior, got out of control when he realized that he was going to take second place to Aeneas? Turnus is one of the most important characters in the second half of the Aeneid. You should think about what makes him tick as you read. Is he a victim or is he to blame for much of the violence that follows?

Finally Allecto has to whip the Trojans up. Ascanius is out hunting, and she puts his dogs on the scent of a deer that turns out to be the pet of one of the Latin families. When Ascanius wounds the deer and it comes creeping back to the family, they fly into a rage and go after Ascanius with clubs and axes. (Once again we see the image of a wounded deer. Even though the hunter didn't mean to hurt this particular deer, its wound brings trouble.) Naturally, the Trojans rush to the rescue of their leader's son, and a huge brawl begins. In the uproar a young boy and an old man, who were trying to calm the people, are both killed.

Allecto reports to Juno on what she has done and asks whether Juno wants her to do anything more, but Juno tells her to go home. Things have gotten so out of control that the human beings won't be able to stop the bloodshed now, and Juno can manage quite nicely alone. When Latinus sees what's become of his plan, he gives up and locks himself in his castle. Because he won't declare war, Juno pushes the iron gates open herself. (The Romans of Virgil's time would have understood this symbol. When they formally declared war, they opened a pair of huge iron gates that stood in the middle of Rome and were dedicated to Mars, the god of war.)

Juno recognizes an important truth here, one which will be an important theme in the second half of the *Aeneid*. Once anger starts, once men begin to be violent, it's very hard for anyone to restore order and peace. Later on, we will even see Aeneas fall victim to uncontrollable rage.

Book VII ends with Turnus gathering an impressive force of his fiercest warriors. There is even a warrior maiden, Camilla, renowned for her strength and skill. But the greatest, strongest, and tallest of them all is Turnus, leading his men in shining armor. (Turnus' troops are called Rutulians.)

BOOK VIII

If you were Aeneas what would you do now? You might be tempted to jump in your boat and try somewhere else—some place a little less hostile. Aeneas is worried and paces by the riverbank. The odds are against him. Turnus has many more men than he does. But then Tiber, the god of the river, speaks to him and reassures him that the Trojans do belong in Latium, and that Ascanius will build a city there, in thirty years, and name it Alba Longa. Then the god tells Aeneas that if he follows the river upstream, he will come to a city named Pallanteum, where he will find allies.

The Trojans row all day and all night until they come to the city of Pallanteum. Its king is named Evander and his son, Pallas, is guarding the banks when they arrive because the people of Pallanteum have been warring against the Latins for a long time and fear invasion. But when Pallas discovers that Aeneas is a Trojan, he welcomes him and quickly brings him to meet his father. It turns out that Evander once was a friend of Anchises, so he's delighted to meet Anchises' son.

NOTE: Evander came from Greece originally, so it seems surprising that he's willing to help the Trojans. Virgil may be saying that in this new alliance the old conflict between Troy and Greece will finally end. Why? One reason might be that the Romans of Virgil's time respected Greek culture and didn't want to think that the Greeks were their enemies. (In fact, they weren't by that time.)

On the day that the Trojans arrive, Pallanteum is the site of an annual festival in honor of Hercules. (Hercules, as you probably know already, was a great Greek hero with terrific strength.) Evander invites the Trojans to join the feast. While they eat, he tells Aeneas how the festival began. Cacus, a terrible creature who was half man and half monster, once terrorized the city. He used to murder men and leave their skins hanging outside his cave on a nearby mountain. Nobody could stop him. Then one day Hercules came by, driving his huge herd of bulls, and Cacus stole some animals and hid them in his cave. Hercules heard them lowing as he went by and became enraged at Cacus. Although Cacus escaped into his cave and sealed it with a huge boulder, Hercules managed to rip off the top of the mountain, exposing Cacus in his lair. Hercules jumped in and strangled him.

You're probably thinking, that's a nice story but what has it to do with Aeneas? Quite a bit. Cacus is another of those creatures that represent rage and disorder. Notice that Hercules gets rid of Cacus and restores peace and order to the city because he's intensely furious. That's part of what gives Hercules so much strength. But Hercules' anger seems justified and we feel no sympathy for horrible Cacus.

Thus, we see that sometimes rage (and war) can be right. If someone attacks you, do you have to keep your temper? Is it ever all right to kill that person? Later on you'll see that Aeneas becomes intensely furious at Turnus for all the bloodshed his anger has caused. You'll have to decide then whether you think Aeneas' anger—and what he does—are as justified as Hercules' was.

After the feast ends, Evander gives Aeneas a short tour of Pallanteum. Pallanteum was built on the very spot where Rome would rise many years later. But what a difference there is between the two cities! Virgil must have amused his fellow Romans by telling them that cows were grazing in the area that became the Roman forum, the "fashionable section" of the city. Then Evander brings Aeneas to a small log cabin where Hercules once slept. (Once again we are told to compare Hercules and Aeneas.) Aeneas settles down contentedly to sleep on a bed of leaves.

NOTE: The emperor Augustus worried that the Romans would get "soft" and lazy because they were so rich and powerful. Have your parents ever told you that you have it easy compared with the way it was for them when they were young? For example, many Romans disapproved of Cleopatra and her luxurious Eastern court. (Dido's beautiful palace was probably modeled on Cleopatra's.) Virgil is showing us that Aeneas, who refused to stay in the luxurious splendor offered by Dido, knows how to rough it.

Meanwhile Venus, always the concerned mother, is worried about the upcoming war with Turnus. She goes to her husband, Vulcan, and sweetly wrapping her arms around him, asks him for a favor. She wants him to make weapons for Aeneas. (Vulcan has a forge underneath the earth where he and his workmen make weapons for the gods.) Vulcan tells Venus that he'd do anything for her; all she has to do is ask. He tells his workmen to drop whatever they're doing and start making some fantastic weapons for Aeneas.

Aeneas and Evander both awaken early the next morning and talk about the war. Evander promises Aeneas all the help he can give, but that isn't much because Pallanteum is poor and small. However, he does tell Aeneas about some other people who are sure to help him. The Etruscans (one of the first civilizations in Italy) are trying to overthrow a terrible tyrant, Mezentius, who is allied with Turnus. However, the prophets have told the Etruscans that they won't succeed unless they have a foreign leader. This sounds like it might be Aeneas!

The old king gives Aeneas 400 of his best men and horses and even sends along his son Pallas, so that Pallas can learn from Aeneas how to be a soldier. As he watches them ride away, he prays that he may live if Pallas lives but that he would rather die than hear that his son has been killed.

That night while the Trojans are camped near the Etruscans, Venus comes to Aeneas with the weapons Vulcan has made. Aeneas picks them up and turns them over carefully. They're so magnificent that he can't believe his eyes. There is a helmet decorated with plumes and flame, a sword and breast-plate made of bronze, and a strong spear. But the best creation of all is a giant shield. Here Vulcan has carved the story of all the great battles and warriors in Rome's future. In the very center are scenes from the Battle of Actium, where Augustus defeated Antony and Cleopatra and ended the civil wars that had plagued Rome. There is even a picture of Augustus marching triumphantly into Rome.

> All this Aeneas
> Sees on his mother's gift, the shield of Vulcan,
> And, without understanding, is proud and
>   happy
> As he lifts to his shoulder all that fortune,
> The fame and glory of his children's children.
>   *(VIII. 728-31)*

NOTE: Here is another example of how Virgil blends the past and present by having Aeneas see the future. Why do you think the Battle of Actium and Augustus' triumph are the most important scenes on the shield? Virgil is suggesting how much Aeneas and Augustus are alike. After all, what's happening in Latium is very much like a civil war—people who could have been living together in peace are fighting each other. If Aeneas can win the war and bring peace and order, it will be just like Augustus' victory at Actium.

In the *Iliad*, Homer described a shield that the gods made for Achilles. Virgil's scene deliberately imitates that description—with some important differences. Achilles' shield showed scenes from everyday life; Aeneas' shows the great events of Rome's military history. This illustrates one of the big differences between the two epics. The *Iliad* is mostly about great individuals and their accomplishments. The *Aeneid*, on the other hand, deals with the successes of a nation. It is a patriotic poem.

This is only one of the many ways in which the second half of the *Aeneid* (Books VI–XII) can be compared with the *Iliad*. The *Iliad* was about the Trojan War. Virgil imitated many of its scenes in describing the battle for Latium in the *Aeneid*. For example, you have already seen how Aeneas can be compared with Paris. As you read, see how many other parallels you can find with the Trojan War.

BOOK IX

You can imagine what Turnus does while Aeneas looks for allies. He attacks the Trojans, of course.

Turnus is the star of Book IX. He's handsome, brave, even funny at times. He's fighting to defend his country against foreign invaders. Wouldn't you do the same? But wasn't Turnus supposed to be a villain? How come Virgil makes him look so good? That's one of the reasons the *Aeneid* is such a great story. Virgil didn't just write a fairy tale with the heroes on one side and the villains on the other. He's showing us that there are good and bad qualities in everybody. When you see how many good qualities Turnus has, you begin to care about him and what happens to him.

You've probably met someone like Turnus at some point in your life. He's the type of person who thinks he can do anything—and he's usually right. He's captain of the football team, president of the student council, and a straight A student. Does he have any faults? Like many people who are this successful, Turnus isn't modest. He brags; he's overconfident and that makes him reckless. Because it never occurs to Turnus that he might fail at anything, he bites off more than he can chew.

We know something else about Turnus. Because of what Allecto did to him, he's out of control with passion for war. Like Juno, he's fighting against fate and he has no chance to win. His insistence on fighting this war only causes pointless bloodshed. He's a force of anger and destruction that we've seen before.

There's Turnus prancing back and forth on his white charger in front of the Trojan camp. Virgil compares him to a wolf pacing outside a sheep pen. Before Aeneas left, the Trojans built walls around the camp so it looks like a fort. Then he gave his soldiers strict instructions not to go outside the walls to attack but only to defend themselves, if Turnus attacked them. Turnus is taunting the Trojans for being cowards and refusing to come out and fight fairly. They follow Aeneas' orders, even though they'd love to show Turnus he's wrong. (For the Trojans this must have been a terrible reminder of being trapped inside the walls of Troy with the Greeks waiting outside!)

Turnus decides to force the Trojans out. He'll set fire to their ships. But when Turnus and his men throw torches at the ships, they magically break loose from their moorings and dive into the water, only to reappear as mermaids! The men are frightened. Even Turnus is a bit surprised, but he decides that this is a good omen. The Trojans' ships are gone. They can never escape.

NOTE: The ships are saved because they were built from trees sacred to the goddess Cybele. She made a deal with Jupiter that the Trojans could have the wood if Jupiter promised that the ships would be turned into goddesses as soon as the Trojans no longer needed them. So Turnus has misinterpreted this omen. It really means that the Trojans are in Italy to stay.

The day ends with Turnus bragging that he is better than the Greeks were in the Trojan War. He won't need a trick like the Trojan Horse to get inside the fort. He'll simply burn and batter the walls until the Trojans surrender. As night falls he posts sentries all around the Trojan camp, while the rest of his men relax around their campfires, drinking and eating. Trapped inside their walls, the Trojans watch the campfires and worry. Where is Aeneas? When will he get back? How long can they hold out?

Nisus and Euryalus are standing watch at the walls. (You've met these two earlier. Remember the footrace in Book V where Nisus tripped the competition so Euryalus could win?) Nisus can't bear to stand around waiting for something to happen. He wants to be a hero. So he and Euryalus devise a bold scheme to sneak through the enemy lines in the dark of night and take a message to Aeneas.

> Euryalus, what is it?
> Do the gods put this ardor in our hearts
> Or does each man's desire become his god?
> *(IX 184-85)*

NOTE: Nisus puts into words one of the important themes that Virgil has hinted at before. Do men do what they do because the gods make them do it? Or is the truth that these impulses already exist in men, and men turn their impulses into gods? For example, do you think Turnus is eager for war because he was infected by an evil force, Allecto? Do you think that fighting is in his blood and he's let the impulse get out of control?

The Trojans are delighted that Nisus and Euryalus are so brave. They sneak through the enemy lines. Suddenly Nisus is carried away by the chance to kill some of the enemy, and he starts to slaughter the sleeping men in his path. Virgil describes him as a hungry lion gorging itself in a sheep pen. (This

description is very similar to the one used earlier for
Turnus.) Euryalus is excited by his friend's success
and he also goes wild, not only killing but grabbing
loot from the dead bodies. Suddenly Nisus remembers that they are supposed to be taking a message to
Aeneas. But Euryalus can't resist grabbing one more
thing—a great golden helmet—and this will be his
downfall. Because they have wasted too much time,
the Rutulians discover them. They see Euryalus' gold-
en helmet flashing through the trees as he tries to run
away. Nisus goes back to try to help his friend, even
though he's vastly outnumbered. The Rutulians kill
them both and put their heads on stakes for the Trojan camp to see.

In this scene Virgil gives us a lesson in true Roman
virtues. Nisus' loyalty to his friend was fine in the
footrace, but here it would have been better if he had
thought of his country first and kept on to Aeneas.
There was nothing he could do to help Euryalus anyway. You should notice, too, how Euryalus' desire for
one more piece of loot destroys him. His greed dis-
tracts him from the real purpose of his mission: to
reach Aeneas. Euryalus is more interested in getting
prizes for himself than in helping his country. In Virgil's view, a good soldier doesn't act for selfish reasons but only for his country. You'll see this theme
again later on.

In the last part of Book IX, Turnus shows his great
skill as a warrior. First he burns down one of the Trojan towers. Then the Trojans, who are guarding their
gates, make a terrible mistake and decide to open
them to lure the enemy in. Turnus rushes in, killing
men in all directions. Fortunately the Trojans are able
to close the gates again before too many more Rutulians get in. But for a while Turnus is unstoppable and

the Trojans are in despair. Finally they realize that
Turnus is only one man and they cannot let themselves be beaten so easily. Surrounded and outnumbered, Turnus leaps over the walls and jumps into the
Tiber and cheerfully swims away, pleased with a
good day's work.

BOOK X

Book X describes the ferocious battle between the
Trojans and the Italians. (The Italians are all the people fighting the Trojans, including the Rutulians, the
Latins, and their allies.) It's one of the best war stories
you'll ever read, full of action and suspense. There are
scenes of bravery and loyalty, cowardice and cruelty.
Virgil shows you both the heroic side of war and its
terrible brutality.

When the Book opens, Jupiter has summoned a
council of the gods. He wants to know why the Trojans and the Italians are fighting. Of course, Venus
blames Juno. Juno answers that it isn't her fault
because she wasn't the one who drove the Trojans
from Troy in the first place. All the gods start blaming
each other and a big fight breaks out. Finally, Jupiter
has had enough and tells them to calm down. From
now on, he orders, no one is to favor either side. Men,
by their own luck and ability, will have to resolve matters on their own. Fate will be revealed without the
gods' intervention.

NOTE: Why do the gods withdraw from the
scene? For one thing, they've certainly made a mess of
everything. But more importantly, Virgil wants you to
focus on the individuals involved, on the rights and
wrongs of what they do on their own. We've seen this

idea before in Virgil. The gods may start the action, but men always have to resolve matters in the end.

Aeneas returns by ship with a fleet of Etruscan allies. He first appears high on the stern of his ship, holding his great shield before him. It glints in the sun. The Trojans holding the fort give a wild whoop of joy. Aeneas is first off the boat and Turnus' troops are already on the beach to meet them.

Although Virgil describes many battles and killings, you should pay the most attention to two of them. In the first, we see young Pallas scoring many victories. (Remember that Pallas is Evander's son and the old man entrusted him to Aeneas. Aeneas feels a special responsibility for the boy, almost as though he were his own son.) Finally, Pallas goes after Lausus, the son of Mezentius (the tyrant and one of Turnus' greatest allies). Lausus is losing the fight and Turnus charges over to help him, like a lion stalking its prey. Although the match is grossly uneven, Pallas bravely throws his spear at Turnus. It barely grazes Turnus. Then Turnus throws his spear, taunting the boy with "Which pierces deeper, Your spear or mine?" The spear goes right through the boy's shield and pierces his chest. Pallas doubles over, belching blood, and dies. Gloating over his victory, Turnus stands with his foot on the body and snatches a beautiful metal belt that Pallas had worn. (If you remember how Euryalus met his downfall by looting the bodies of his victims, you'll begin to suspect that Turnus may regret this move.)

When Aeneas finds out what has happened, he flies into a rage and we see a great change in how he fights. Before this he was fierce, but now he's furious and doesn't spare anyone in his path. However, he's

out to get Turnus in particular. Aeneas seems a bit out
of control himself in these scenes.

At this point Juno becomes truly depressed, for she
realizes that the end is coming soon. (From this point
on you'll see that Juno seems less angry and more
depressed. You can understand why—all her
schemes have failed. But it wouldn't be like Juno to
give up completely.) She asks Jupiter's permission to
delay the end a little longer. She tricks Turnus into
chasing a ghost of Aeneas, and gets him away from
the action and out of danger. For once it seems that
Juno is preventing violence. However, the truth is
that her delaying tactics only prolong the killing and
chaos. Once again we see that Juno's irrational behav-
ior is always destructive.

Now that Turnus is chasing a ghost of Aeneas, we
get a good look at Aeneas in action, and we see the
second important scene in this Book. Aeneas fights
the tyrant Mezentius and wounds him badly. Lausus
rushes in to help his father. Aeneas realizes that the
boy has no chance and warns him away, but the son
won't abandon his father. Finally, Aeneas loses his
patience and drives his sword through the boy's
body.

> And now
> Aeneas changes. Looking on that face
> So pale in death, he groans in pity; he reaches
> As if to touch him with his hand, in comfort
> Knowing, himself, how one can love a father.
> 'Poor boy, what tribute can Aeneas offer,
> What praise for so much glory? Keep the armor
> You loved so much'
>
> (X. 815-20)

With that he gently lifts the body from the ground
and gives it to Lausus' companions for burial.

Do you see how differently Aeneas and Turnus act in these two scenes? Both were involved in uneven contests between men and boys, but Turnus attacked Pallas while Aeneas tried to warn Lausus away. After he wins, Turnus gloats and snatches a trophy from the boy's body. He feels no remorse, no pity. But Aeneas is almost horrified by what he's done. He remembers how much he loved his own father, Anchises, and how he would have done anything to help him. He doesn't blame Lausus for defending his father. He doesn't steal anything from Lausus' body, but hands it over gently to his comrades.

You begin to see that Aeneas is different—and greater—than Turnus. It's not because he's a better warrior or more exciting—he's not. But Aeneas is able to understand and respect his enemy. He can feel pity. Aeneas isn't simple-minded. He doesn't think war is fun. He realizes what a terrible waste it can be. In these scenes we see what a Roman soldier should be. He does his duty; he's not afraid to kill when he has to. But he's not out of control. He knows how to restrain himself and can respect the other side.

NOTE: A virtue that the Romans of Virgil's time emphasized was that of love and respect between father and son. We've already seen a good example of this in the relationship between Aeneas and Anchises. But the Romans also believed in loyalty to one's country. When Aeneas decides to kill Lausus, he must make a terrible choice between these two virtues. Although he would like to respect Lausus' devotion to his father, his duty to his country is to kill both father and son. For Aeneas, duty to his country always wins. Here is another example of how the *Aeneid* is a patriotic poem.

BOOK XI

The dead, both Trojan and Italian, are scattered all over the fields. The women wail over the bodies of their husbands and sons. Everywhere smoke rises from the funeral pyres. In Book X, we saw the violence and sometimes the glory of war. In Book XI, Virgil shows the terrible sorrow and waste war leaves behind.

The Latin people are beginning to doubt that this war is a very good idea after all. They send a delegation to Aeneas to ask for a truce so that they can bury their dead. Aeneas is happy to grant it. He never wanted to fight in the first place, but Turnus insisted. Aeneas proposes a solution—he and Turnus should fight alone. The Trojans will either stay or leave, depending on who wins.

Aeneas is a wise and sensible leader here. He doesn't want more innocent people to suffer. He is trying to restore order, but that won't be easy to accomplish.

Meanwhile a funeral procession returns Pallas' body to Evander, who rushes from his house, wild with grief. He protests that the gods have not granted his wish to die before his son. Now he must live with this terrible sorrow. But he gives the Trojans a message for Aeneas: although Evander will never be happy again, he will be satisfied when he hears that Turnus has been killed for slaying Pallas.

Latinus holds a meeting of his leading citizens to discuss Aeneas' proposal. As they are debating, word comes that one of their last hopes, help from a Greek named Diomede, has fallen through. Diomede says that he no longer has a reason to fight the Trojans and besides, Aeneas is too great to fight. Therefore, Latinus would like to make peace. The kingdom is large enough to give a part to the Trojans. A senator named Drances, also in favor of peace, supports Latinus' plan. But Drances is also terribly jealous of the strong and brave Turnus. So, as he speaks he taunts Turnus, suggesting that he is not brave enough to face Aeneas alone. Knowing Turnus, you can imagine that he won't accept Drances' speech. He starts to rant and rave. Drances is a good talker, he says, but when it comes to fighting, he's hiding out in the senate house. Then he goes on to appeal to the other Latin leaders. Don't give up so easily! The Latins are on the edge of winning! All they need to do is try again!

Turnus gets his wish for more fighting because at that moment the news arrives that the Trojans are approaching the city. The people panic. Turnus jumps into his armor and charges off. Virgil compares him to a stallion who has just broken its tether and dashes from the stable, rushing to the pastures or splashing in the river in sheer joy. The stallion is beautiful and free, full of energy. There is something wonderful about Turnus, his strength, his confidence. But there's another side to this image. The stallion doesn't know what it's doing or why. It just bolts for freedom. It has no judgment. A good leader should have more sense.

NOTE: Many readers have complained that Aeneas is a rather dull character. He means well, and he's courageous, but he's not very exciting. Remember how he behaved with Dido? He couldn't even argue with her. He just said he had to do what the gods told him to do. Can you see Turnus acting like that?

But Virgil is trying to tell us something about the qualities that make up a good leader. They're not necessarily show-stoppers. In addition to strength and bravery, a good leader must have sound judgment, be moderate and calm, and have respect for the gods and for his fellow man.

You might be interested to know that Augustus had a reputation for being cold and aloof. Perhaps Virgil's description of Aeneas is a defense of Augustus.

The warrior maiden, Camilla, offers to help Turnus. She will lead the cavalry while Turnus hides in a narrow pass, waiting to ambush Aeneas. Camilla performs brilliantly for a while but then makes a mistake we've seen before. While she's craving the gorgeous armor of a Trojan warrior, another Trojan sneaks up behind her and shoots her with his arrow. (Because Camilla is sacred to the goddess Diana, the poor Trojan also has to die.)

Without Camilla, the Italian cavalry is routed by the Trojans, who rush to attack the Latin city. As the Trojans pour through the gates and over the walls, even the women and children try desperately to fight them off. Do you see how the roles have reversed since the fall of Troy? Now the Trojans are doing to the Latins what the Greeks did to Troy.

Turnus, hearing the screaming and seeing the smoke from the burning city, rushes from his hiding spot to return to the city to help. But here he makes a terrible mistake. If he had only waited a few minutes more, Aeneas would have come through the pass and Turnus could have killed him.

BOOK XII

Everything you've been reading and thinking about comes together in Book XII, which contains the climax of the *Aeneid*. All the major themes are found here:

fate and the gods, the effect of uncontrolled anger, the kind of person Aeneas is, the kind of nation Rome will be.

Do you think it's ever right to kill someone? If you're a pacifist, you don't think it's ever right and you've probably been rather disturbed by all the violence needed to found Rome. On the other hand, you may think that there are some situations where it is right to kill someone. How do you feel about capital punishment? If someone murders innocent people, should that person be put to death? What if the murderer is insane? Does that make any difference?

And what about war? When is a war justified? Most people feel that there is something basically different between killing someone for your own private reasons, and fighting for your country. But what makes it different? What is the relationship between a person's responsibility to his country and his responsibility to his fellow man?

These are the difficult questions that Virgil raised in Book XII for his Roman audience—and for you—to think about. Your personal reaction to the final terrible struggle between Aeneas and Turnus will help you decide what you think is right.

When Turnus realizes that his troops are beaten, he finally accepts the fact that he must battle Aeneas directly. He tells Latinus to go ahead with the plan for a truce between the two armies so that the two leaders can battle it out alone.

Both Latinus and his wife, Amata, beg Turnus to give up the fight. Amata becomes hysterical, saying that she'll kill herself if Turnus dies and her daughter must marry Aeneas. (Allecto's poison is still at work in Amata.) But their pleas only make Turnus more furious. As you can see, Turnus is now completely alone in his rage for battle. Virgil compares Turnus to a raging lion who has been wounded but who fights all the harder because it's a lost cause. There's no point to the battle, but Turnus has never known when to stop.

The truce is arranged, and the Italians gather on one side of a huge field and the Trojans on the other to watch the final battle between their great leaders. An altar is built, and sacrifices to the gods are made ready to honor the winner. Aeneas prays to the gods (including Juno) and swears that if he loses, the Trojans will leave Italy forever. He also promises that if he wins, he will treat the Italians as equals of the Trojans. He does not want to conquer the Italians, he wants peace on equal terms.

We see here what a good and just leader Aeneas has become. Even after all this bloodshed, he is not angry and does not want revenge. (You might think back to Anchises' prediction in Book VI that the Romans' great skill will be the art of ruling.)

But Juno still has a hard time accepting fate. Although Jupiter has forbidden the gods to interfere anymore, Juno invents a way to get around his rule. Turnus' sister is a nymph named Juturna. Juno goes to her and asks her to help Turnus.

Juturna, disguising herself as one of the Italians, goes among the crowd, whispering that it isn't fair that Turnus should have to fight this one out all by himself. The Italians are already uneasy; it looks like Aeneas might win. One of them hurls his spear into the Trojan ranks. The Trojans go wild and bedlam breaks out. Spears and arrows fly from all sides. Aeneas tries to stop the fighting, crying out that the battle is for him alone, but no one listens. Then a flying arrow wounds him in the leg.

Turnus, seeing Aeneas being carried off the field, is

delighted. Now the Italians have another chance to fight for victory. He jumps into his chariot and races across the field, spearing Trojans wherever he sees them and hanging their heads from his chariot as trophies.

Do you see the difference between Turnus and Aeneas? Aeneas tries to control the crowd. He wants an orderly battle between Turnus and himself. This will cost the least loss of life. But Turnus is always eager for war, and instead of trying to calm his troops and honor the truce, he leads them into a new battle. His actions create more disorder.

Aeneas is frantic that he cannot stop Turnus, but his wound keeps him from walking. At first his doctor cannot remove the arrow, but then Venus gives the doctor a magic potion that releases the arrow and eases the pain.

NOTE: Why is Venus allowed to interfere like this? She's not really tipping the balance in Aeneas' favor. She's just evening the score after what Juturna did.

Now Aeneas puts on his mighty armor and thunders across the field, determined to hunt Turnus down. Knowing this, Juturna disguises herself as the driver of Turnus' chariot and drives erratically around the field. Aeneas on foot, and with a wounded leg, can't possibly catch up.

NOTE: If you think of Juno and Juturna as symbols for impulses that already exist in Turnus, you might begin to think that Turnus is avoiding Aeneas. Is he afraid? After all his bragging, is he really a coward?

Aeneas then thinks of a way to force Turnus to fight. He turns his Trojan army against the city and begins setting fire to the walls. When Amata realizes that the city is under attack, she mistakenly concludes that Turnus must be dead and she kills herself. Latinus is left in despair at the death of his wife and the failure of all his efforts at peace.

NOTE: Latinus certainly hasn't been a very effective leader. Virgil may be hinting that the Latins desperately need new leadership. This helps justify the Trojan "invasion."

Turnus hears the wailing and crying from the city and finally stops his insane flight over the battlefield. Recognizing his sister's tricks, he tells her to stop. He realizes that he must go to the defense of his city and that his people are suffering because of his refusal to fight Aeneas. Although some sense of responsibility seems to dawn on Turnus at this point, it appears very late.

Aeneas turns to meet Turnus at last. Turnus strikes a mighty blow with his sword. But, in his frenzy to get to the battle that morning, he took the wrong sword and it breaks on Aeneas' shield.

Turnus has no choice but to race away with Aeneas in hot pursuit. But Aeneas is slower because of his wound. He tries to catch Turnus with his spear, but he misses and the spear lands in a tree. Aeneas cannot pull it out. Juturna gives Turnus his good sword and, once again, Venus restores the balance by freeing Aeneas' spear.

At last Jupiter has had enough, and he orders Juno to stop making trouble in any way. Miraculously,

Juno accepts this order quietly. All she asks is that the Trojan name die and both the Italians and Trojans be known as Latins. Juno's anger has finally worked itself out, and now Troy is extinct. The Trojans have a new identity. They are free to start again without an angry goddess pursuing them.

NOTE: Isn't this a rather realistic description of how anger stops? Have you ever been really furious? You rant and rave. You may even do some destructive (or self-destructive) things. Finally, you just stop being angry. It's a relief that Juno finally feels better, but she's left Aeneas and Turnus with the consequences. They still have to resolve the anger in themselves.

The end comes at last. Aeneas aims his spear and Turnus falls to the ground, wounded in the thigh. Aeneas rushes up, his sword poised, ready to strike. Turnus speaks his last words:

> I have deserved it, surely,
> And I do not beg off. Use the advantage.
> But if a parent's grief has any power
> To touch the spirit, I pray you, pity Daunus,
> (I would Anchises), send him back my body.
> You have won; I am beaten, and these hands go
>   out
> In supplication: everyone has seen it.
> No more. I have lost Lavinia. Let hatred
> Proceed no further.
>
> (XII. 930-37)

Aeneas pauses for a moment, almost moved to spare Turnus. But then he sees that Turnus is wearing the belt he stole from Pallas and he plunges his sword through Turnus.

How do you feel about Aeneas now? The last thing you see him do is kill a defenseless man. It's hard not to feel terribly sorry for Turnus. It takes courage to admit you were wrong. And it's not so clear that Turnus was entirely to blame for everything that happened. Has Aeneas just been infected with the uncontrollable rage that has caused him so much trouble all through the *Aeneid*? Some readers think so, and they think that Virgil's final judgment on the Roman Empire was a very dark one: that its success was rooted in this kind of violence.

But we can look at this another way. Aeneas does pity Turnus in that last moment before he strikes. But when he sees Pallas' belt, he remembers all the needless bloodshed that Turnus' madness has caused. How does he know that if he lets Turnus live that Turnus will really change his ways? Maybe Turnus only says what he does in the hope that Aeneas will spare his life. In the end, Aeneas chooses order and the safety of his country over his feeling for another, and in many ways great, man.

Virgil wrote the *Aeneid* at the end of the Roman civil wars. Augustus killed many of his rivals in order to restore order. Was Augustus right? Was Aeneas right? Virgil's sad and troubling ending leaves the decision up to you.

A STEP BEYOND

Tests and Answers

TESTS

Test 1

1. In 31 B.C., Virgil finally felt hope for his _____
   country when
   A. Julius Caesar was assassinated
   B. he left Rome and went to Naples
   C. Augustus ended the civil wars

2. Aeneas is meant to represent _____
   A. Julius Caesar
   B. Marc Antony
   C. Augustus Caesar

3. The Trojans' enemy among the gods is _____
   A. Juno
   B. Venus
   C. Jupiter

4. Aeneas is motivated most by _____
   A. fate
   B. a sense of duty
   C. fierce ambition

5. The Queen of Carthage is _____
   A. Dido
   B. Creusa
   C. Lavinia

6. A flashback about the fall of Troy occurs when _____
   Aeneas
   A. tells Dido of his past
   B. meets Anchises in the Underworld
   C. is welcomed to Italy by Latinus

7. Virgil shows that the Trojans were only _____ defeated by
   A. their own cowardice
   B. treachery and deceit
   C. superior military strategy

8. Aeneas wanders for years, just like Homer's _____ hero
   A. Hector
   B. Achilles
   C. Odysseus

9. Allecto is sent by Juno to _____
   A. whip up thoughts of war
   B. calm the angry Latins
   C. make Aeneas fall in love with Lavinia

10. Turnus' great flaw is that _____
    A. his passion for war is out of control
    B. he is a weak soldier
    C. he falls in love with a woman

11. What qualities make Aeneas a great leader?

12. Discuss how Aeneas' travels in the first six books of the *Aeneid* represent a voyage of self-discovery.

13. Do you like Aeneas or Dido better? Why?

14. Why does Aeneas kill Turnus? Was it the right thing to do?

15. Compare Dido and Turnus. How are they similar? How are they different?

Test 2

1. Virgil wanted to tell the story of the founding _____ of the Roman Empire because
   A. he felt the Empire had gone downhill

B. he believed Augustus was destined to rule the world

C. the Romans destroyed Carthage

2. Two major subjects of the *Aeneid* are _____
   A. fate and duty
   B. arms and the man
   C. war and peace

3. Julius Caesar claimed that he was descended _____ from
   A. Jupiter
   B. Latinus
   C. Aeneas

4. Juno's favorite city is _____
   A. Troy
   B. Carthage
   C. Rome

5. Dido fell in love with Aeneas because _____
   A. Cupid shot her with an arrow
   B. they were both exiles
   C. Juno wanted to keep him in Carthage

6. Aeneas ran away from Troy because _____
   A. he was told in a dream to find a second Troy
   B. his father begged him to go
   C. he was disillusioned with Troy's leaders

7. Aeneas gets a vision of the future of Rome _____ when
   A. Dido shows him her tapestry in Carthage
   B. he visits Anchises in the Underworld
   C. Evander welcomes him in Italy

8. A pair of close friends are _____
   A. Turnus and Pallas

   B. Aeneas and Ascanius
   C. Nisus and Euryalus

9. Aeneas is similar to Homer's hero Achilles   _____
  when
   A. he mourns his father
   B. he receives a magnificent shield from the
     gods
   C. he goes to the Underworld

10. Rome was built on the site of: _____
    I. Troy
    II. Pallanteum
    III. Latium
    A. I and II only   B. II and III only   C. I, II, and III

11. Discuss the relationship between anger and disorder in the *Aeneid*.

12. What is the role of fate in the *Aeneid*?

13. What is the relationship between the gods and men?

14. Discuss how Virgil uses fire as a symbol of destruction.

15. The *Aeneid* is an epic about Rome. Discuss.

ANSWERS

Test 1

1. C   2. C   3. A   4. B   5. A   6. A
7. B   8. C   9. A   10. A

    11. The first quality you would mention is Aeneas' strong sense of duty to his family, fellow Trojans, and the gods. Part of this quality is his complete lack of selfishness. For example, in Book II he carries his father, Anchises, out of Troy on his back. In Book IV he leaves Dido and all the

happiness he had with her for the sake of his son and his country's future. Throughout, Aeneas always prays to the gods and obeys them. One result is that they help him. For example, Jupiter puts out the fire on the Trojan ships in Book V.

Another quality you would discuss is Aeneas' great strength, skill, and bravery as a warrior. These are shown especially in the last four Books. You would point out that Aeneas always acts with moderation, even in war. He is never unnecessarily brutal, but when he has to kill, he can. (See Books X and XII.)

You would also point out Aeneas' skill in reaching compromises and keeping order. For example, in Book V you see him award prizes to all the contestants in the funeral games so that everybody remains happy. In Books XI and XII you see that Aeneas is willing to fight Turnus alone to prevent unnecessary bloodshed.

You could conclude by noting that all these qualities enable Aeneas to bring peace and order to Italy. Thus, he is the model for a perfect Roman leader.

12. You could answer this question by showing how in Book I Aeneas wishes that he had died in Troy, instead of being stuck in a storm at sea. His heart is still in the past. In Book II, he wants to fight even though Troy is doomed. He leaves only because the gods tell him to. Then you could show how his travels in Book III illustrate how, at first, he has no idea of his destination. He keeps making mistakes and relying on his father, who doesn't know any better than he does. He doesn't make his own decisions until Anchises dies.

Aeneas' stop in Buthrotum in Book III is the first indication that he is beginning to accept the necessity of change. Buthrotum is just like Troy and Aeneas could stay there but he leaves because he realizes that his fate is to build a completely new city. In Book IV Aeneas makes an important discovery about his emotions. He leaves Dido because he realizes that the future of his country and obedience to the gods are more important to him than love. Finally in Book VI, when Aeneas journeys to the underworld and sees the future of Rome, he becomes inspired by the future and is convinced that all his struggles are worth the effort. He leaves the past and Troy behind.

13. There is neither a right nor a wrong answer to this question. Although it depends on what you feel about the characters, you'll want to be able to explain why you feel the way you do. If you prefer Dido, you'll point out that she seems to be a real person with real feelings. She was generous and kind to Aeneas and his Trojans when they were desperate for help. Her only mistake was to love Aeneas too much. Even that wasn't her fault because Venus and Cupid made her fall in love. You'll also point out how badly Aeneas behaves when he leaves. He starts preparing the fleet before he has even spoken to Dido. When she finds out, he gives her a cold, rational explanation of why he must leave. He never expresses any emotion. It's as if the year they spent together never happened. It's no wonder that she goes crazy with grief and anger. Finally, you'd conclude that her act of killing herself was very courageous.

If you like Aeneas better than Dido, you would emphasize how much strength it must have taken for him to leave her. You would point out that he really did love Dido, but that he had to leave because Jupiter ordered him to go. He had no choice. The reason that he didn't tell Dido was that he was trying to think of a gentle way to break the news. However, she attacked him before he could think of anything and he just told her the simple truth. You could show how much Aeneas really cared for Dido by mentioning the sad and tender way that he greets her when in Book VI he meets her shade in the underworld.

14. There are two possible reasons why Aeneas kills Turnus. First, when he sees the belt that Turnus stole after he killed young Pallas, Aeneas goes wild with rage and can't stop himself from killing, even though Turnus has admitted he was wrong and has asked for an end to hatred. If you think that is why Aeneas kills Turnus, then you'll probably conclude that all the anger and hatred, which started with Juno and has caused so much trouble throughout the *Aeneid*, has finally infected Aeneas. You'll wonder what that means for the future. Is Aeneas now out of control himself? Or is this an isolated act that finally puts an end to the anger? Whatever you decide, you'll probably be left with the uneasy feeling that Virgil is telling us that once violence starts, it's hard, if not impossible, to stop it.

On the other hand, you may decide that Aeneas' decision to kill Turnus is not made in a burst of rage but is a rational one. You'll point out that Aeneas considers sparing Turnus' life, at first, but when he sees Pallas' belt he remembers how much trouble Turnus has caused and how many people have died needlessly because of him. He kills Turnus to punish him and to prevent him from causing any more trouble. This is a tragic decision for Aeneas, but it shows what a firm leader he will be. On a personal level, he feels sympathy for Turnus and would spare him, but as leader of his people he knows that the surest way to set a good example and restore order is to kill Turnus.

15. Dido and Turnus are similar because they are both infected with uncontrolled passion by the gods (Books I and VII). Both are great and noble people. She is a good and kind queen; he is a brave and handsome warrior. But their passions make them both irrational. Dido disregards her reputation and kingdom. Turnus disregards the welfare of his people in his desire to fight at all costs. He makes mistakes because he is so impulsive. (For example, in Book XII, he leaves his ambush spot and rushes off to another battle minutes before Aeneas will arrive.) Both Dido and Turnus are victims of Aeneas' fate. Aeneas must leave Dido; he must settle in Turnus' land. Finally, both characters present the same philosophical question. Did their passions really originate with the gods or are the gods simply symbols for forces that were already inside both of them?

Dido and Turnus are different because their passions are different. Hers is love, which hurts no one but herself. But Turnus' is war, and his recklessness costs many lives. Dido kills herself but Turnus forces Aeneas to kill him. Dido seems to represent the personal and emotional side of life that Aeneas must leave behind in order to build his new kingdom. But Turnus seems to represent the forces of disorder that must be conquered if that kingdom is to survive. That difference makes Dido's fate seem more tragic than Turnus'.

Test 2

1. B   2. B   3. C   4. B   5. A   6. A
7. B   8. C   9. B   10. B

11.   The source of the anger in the *Aeneid* is Juno. She hates the Trojans (Book I). But it isn't her anger alone that creates disorder. Juno's anger creates disorder because it goes against fate. The Trojans are fated to reach Italy and build a new city, but Juno is so angry that she can't stand this idea. Thus, she decides to fight fate, even though there is no way that she can win. All she can do is delay fate by causing trouble. You can see that the way Juno expresses her anger is irrational and that causes disorder. Other examples of uncontrolled anger that lead to disorder are Pyrrhus' attack on Priam (Book II), Dido's fury at Aeneas and decision to kill herself (Book IV), and Turnus' refusal to stop fighting (Book XI).

You might want to point out that not all anger leads to disorder. If the anger is rational, it can be a force for order. You see that when Jupiter loses his patience with the gods for interfering in the Trojans' affairs (Book X), he brings order rather than disorder. Similarly, when Aeneas kills Turnus, his anger ends the trouble that Turnus has caused.

12. Fate is the moving force in the *Aeneid*. From the very beginning of Book I you know that Aeneas must leave Troy and go to Italy because he is compelled by fate. You also know that Aeneas is fated to build a new city and even that the Roman Empire is fated to arise. No one, not even the gods, can change fate.

You'll want to discuss what effect fate has on the way men live their lives. Men must still struggle to discover their fates. Although Aeneas is destined to build his new city, it's a difficult task for him. Sometimes fate seems cruel or unfair. For example, Dido seems to be a victim of a very unlucky fate. Finally, you might want to discuss whether fate makes people the way they are or whether their fates result from the kinds of people they already are. For example, you could argue that Aeneas becomes a great leader because fate forces that role on him. (You could point out how in Books I–III he begins as a terribly unhappy and uncertain leader, but becomes a good leader by the end of the *Aeneid*.) Or you could argue that Aeneas reaches Italy and wins the war because he always had the qualities of a leader: great responsibility, determination, and strength.

13. On a literal level the gods are divine beings who are able to intervene in human affairs. They have personalities very much like human beings but are more powerful. They aren't completely benevolent—they have the same kinds of motivations that people do. For example, Juno becomes angry and vindictive. Venus, who wants her son to succeed, can be tricky and playful. (See Book I.) The only god who seems more like our idea of a god, and less like a normal human being, is Jupiter, who is the king of the gods and more powerful than the others. He doesn't really take sides. He stands for order. He wants everything to go according to fate.

Men must pray to the gods if they want to succeed. For example, in Book V you can see that the boat captain, Cloanthus, wins because he prays to the gods for help. The gods can help or hurt men, but they can't change a man's basic fate.

On a symbolic level you can discuss how the gods seem to represent natural forces. For example, Juno always causes trouble by using natural elements: storms and fires. Other gods seem to represent emotions that exist inside all of us. For example, Cupid (Book I) represents love, while Allecto (Book VII) represents anger and hatred.

14. Virgil uses fire imagery throughout the *Aeneid* to symbolize the destructive power of uncontrolled anger and passion. You could point to Book II where Troy is burning because of the angry attack of the Greeks (and the gods). You might mention how Dido's passion in Books I and IV is described as "burning," and you should talk about her funeral pyre, which Aeneas sees as he's sailing away. In Book V, the Trojan women set fire to the fleet after a goddess sent by Juno whips them into a frenzy. In Book VII, Allecto uses a torch to set Turnus on fire with passion for war and in Book IX, Turnus uses fire twice—once to try to burn the Trojan fleet, and once to burn down part of the Trojan fort.

15. First you would discuss how the *Aeneid* shows the early history of Rome from the fall of Troy in the 12th century B.C. to the first settlement by Aeneas. Then Book VI shows what happened from Aeneas' death to the time of Augustus.

You would also discuss how Virgil uses Aeneas as a model of a great Roman leader. You might also consider Book VIII, where Aeneas visits Evander at the future site of Rome, and learns basic Roman virtues such as the merits of a simple life, strength, and sound political judgment.

Finally you could show how the *Aeneid* reflects Roman political crises that happened during Virgil's time. For example, Aeneas ends the war in Italy just as Augustus ended the civil wars in Rome.

Term Paper Ideas

Aeneas

1. Discuss whether or not Aeneas did the right thing when he left Dido.

2. What do Aeneas and Dido have in common? How are they different?

3. Compare and contrast Aeneas and Turnus as warriors. Pay particular attention to the killings of Pallas and Lausus.

4. Discuss the relationship between Aeneas and his father, Anchises. Is there a symbolic reason why Anchises dies before the Trojans reach Italy?

5. In Book II, why doesn't Aeneas leave Troy immediately? What does this tell you about his values at this point? Do his values remain the same when he's fighting in Italy?

6. Discuss the parade of great Romans Aeneas sees in the underworld and how it affects him.

7. Give an example of how Aeneas represents Augustus.

8. Give three examples of how Venus helps Aeneas. Does she ever do anything that hurts him?

9. In may ways Aeneas is a sad person. Give three examples of things or events that make him sad and discuss why they have this effect.

Dido

1. Give two different explanations for the reason Dido falls in love with Aeneas, and explain which you think is correct.

2. Why does Virgil compare Dido to a wounded deer in Book IV?

3. How does Dido's passion affect her ability to rule?

4. At the end of Book IV, when Dido predicts that there will be war between Carthage and Rome, what wars does she refer to? Who is the great avenger?

5. What historical character might Dido represent? What does this suggest about who Aeneas might represent while he is in Carthage? When he leaves?

Turnus

1. Does Turnus fight for his country or for himself?

2. Give two examples of how Turnus' passion for war always leads to more violence.

3. Why does Virgil compare Turnus to wild animals, like stallions, wolves, and lions (Books IX through XII)? What does that tell you about his character?

The Gods

1. Give an example of how Juno's scheme to prevent the Trojans from reaching Italy backfires.

2. Discuss why Juno is so angry at the Trojans.

3. Why doesn't Juno succeed in preventing the Trojans from reaching Italy and winning the war there?

4. Give two examples of gods who symbolize human passions, and explain their roles in the *Aeneid*.

5. Name two gods who represent the forces of order in the world, and give two examples of how they enforce order.

Miscellaneous

1. Discuss some ways in which the themes that Virgil wrote about in the *Aeneid* reflect the times in which he lived.

2. Give three examples of how the *Aeneid* is similar to the *Iliad* and the *Odyssey*. Give one example of how it is different.

3. Give two examples of epic similes in the *Aeneid*. Pick your favorite and discuss what it tells you about the person's character.

Further Reading

CRITICAL WORKS

Anderson, William S., *The Art of the Aeneid*. Englewood Cliffs: Prentice-Hall, 1969.

Camps, William Anthony, *An Introduction to Virgil's Aeneid*. London: Oxford University Press, 1969.

Commager, Steele, ed., *Virgil: A Collection of Critical Essays*. Englewood Cliffs: Prentice-Hall, 1966.

DiCesare, Mario A., *The Altar and the City*. New York: Columbia University Press, 1974.

Hadas, Moses, *A History of Latin Literature*. New York: Columbia University Press, 1952.

Hamilton, Edith, *The Roman Way*. New York: Norton & Co., 1932.

Hunt, J. William, *Forms of Glory: Structure and Sense in Virgil's Aeneid*. Carbondale and Edwardsville: Southern Illinois University Press, 1973.

Johnson, W. R., *Darkness Visible: A Study of Vergil's Aeneid*. Berkeley: University of California Press, 1976.

Mackail, J.W., *Virgil and His Meaning to the World of Today*. New York: Cooper Square Publishers, 1963.

Ogilvie, Robert Maxwell, *Roman Literature and Society*. New York: Penguin, 1980.

Poschl, Viktor, *The Art of Vergil, Image and Symbol in the Aeneid*. Ann Arbor: University of Michigan Press, 1962.

Tenney, Frank, *Vergil, A Biography*. New York: Russel & Russel, 1965.

A SELECTION OF ENGLISH TRANSLATIONS OF THE AENEID

Dryden, John, *The Aeneid*. New York: Macmillan, 1965. (In verse.)

Fitzgerald, Robert, *The Aeneid*. New York: Random House, 1983. (In verse.)

Humphries, Rolfe, *The Aeneid of Virgil*. New York: Scribners, 1951 (In verse.)

Knight, W. F. Jackson, *Virgil, The Aeneid*. Harmondsworth: Penguin, 1956. (In prose.)

Lewis, C. Day, *Aeneid*. New York: Oxford University Press, 1952. (In verse.)

AUTHOR'S OTHER WORKS

Bovie, S. P. *Virgil's Georgics*. Chicago University Press, 1956. (In verse.)

Johnson, G., *The Pastorals of Vergil*. Lawrence: University of Kansas Press, 1960. (In verse.)

Lewis, C. Day, *Eclogues and Georgics*. Garden City: Anchor Books, 1964 (In verse.)

Glossary

Acestes King of western Sicily who was friendly to the Trojans.

Achaeans Name for the Greeks.

Achaemenides Greek man left behind by Ulysses on Sicily in land of the Cyclopes. Rescued by Trojans in Book III.

Achates Aeneas' faithful companion and armor-bearer.

Acheron One of the rivers of the underworld.

Achilles Greek hero of Homer's *Iliad*; known for his wrath; killed during Trojan War.

Actium Site of Battle of Actium in 31 B.C. in which Augustus defeated Antony and Cleopatra. Briefly visited by Aeneas and Trojans.

Adonis Beautiful youth loved by Aphrodite (Venus).

Aeneadae Another name for the Trojans.

Aeneas Hero of the *Aeneid*.

Aeolus King of the winds.

Ajax Greek hero in Trojan War.

Alba Longa Town near Rome, founded by Aeneas' son Ascanius.

Allecto One of the Furies, used by Juno to incite Turnus to war.

Amata Wife of Latinus, the king of the Latins, and mother of Lavinia. She is poisoned by Allecto and refuses to allow Lavinia to marry Aeneas. She prefers Turnus.

Anchises Aeneas' aged father.

Andromache Hector's wife. After Hector died at Troy, Andromache married Helenus and lived at Buthrotum, one of the places Aeneas visits in Book III.

Anna Dido's sister and confidante.

Apollo God of the sun and able to foretell the future.

Ascanius Aeneas' young son. Also known as Iulus.

Augustus Roman emperor (30 B.C.–14 A.D.).

Aurora Goddess of dawn.

Ausonia Another name for Italy.

Avernus Cave near Cumae where Aeneas enters underworld. Also another name for underworld.

Bacchus God of wine. Also associated with frenzy.

Bellona Roman goddess of war.

Brundisium Place where Virgil died, on east coast of Italy.

Buthrotum On west coast of Greece. Place where Aeneas stops and sees miniature version of Troy and meets Helenus and Andromache

Cacus A horrible, fire-breathing monster that terrorized Pallanteum (the site of Rome). Killed by Hercules.

Caesar The Roman dictator, Julius Caesar. Augustus, who was his adopted son, also used this title.

Caieta Nurse of Aeneas, who dies right before the Trojans reach Latium.

Calaeno The leader of the Harpies who attacks the Trojans in Book III. Prophesies their future in Italy.

Calchas Greek prophet at Troy.

Calliope The Muse of epic poetry.

Camilla Warrior maiden in Italy. Helps Turnus and is slain by Trojans. Sacred to Diana.

Carthage Dido's kingdom in northern Africa.

Cassandra Daughter of Priam, king of Troy. Prophetess fated never to be believed.

Cerberus The three-headed dog of the underworld.

Ceres Roman goddess of agriculture.

Charon Ferryman in the underworld.

Charybdis Sea monster who creates whirlpool that sucks in ships in the strait between Italy and Sicily.

Circe An enchantress encountered by Ulysses in the *Odyssey*. Aeneas avoids her.

Clio Muse of history.

Cloanthus One of the Trojans and captain of a boat in Book V.

Cocytus A river in the underworld.

Creusa Aeneas' wife who dies at Troy.

Cumae City on west coast of Italy where Aeneas meets the Sibyl.

Cupid God of love and son of Venus.

Cyclopes One-eyed monsters in Sicily who liked to eat men.

Daedalus Greek inventor and father of Icarus. Builder of the labyrinth and temple of Apollo at Cumae.

Dardanus A Trojan ancestor who came from Italy.

Dares Trojan boxer defeated by old Sicilian boxer Entellus in Book V.

Deiphobus Son of Priam who married Helen after Paris died and who was brutally murdered by her husband, Menelaus. Aeneas meets his shade in the underworld.

Delos Island in the Aegean Sea, sacred to Apollo. Aeneas visits Delos in Book III.

Diana Twin sister of Apollo; goddess of hunting, moon, and patron of maidens. See Camilla.

Dido Queen of Carthage, who fell passionately in love with Aeneas and committed suicide when he left.

Diomedes One of the Greek heroes at Troy. Later a king in Italy whom Turnus asks for help.

Dis King of the underworld.

Drances Latin senator who tries to make peace between Trojans and Latins and who hates Turnus.

Drepanum Modern Trapani. Place in Sicily where Trojans land and have funeral games to honor Anchises.

Elissa Another name for Dido.

Elysian Fields The place in the underworld where good souls stay.

Entellus Old Sicilian boxer who defeats Dares.

Epirus Region in western Greece where Trojans land.

Erebus Another name for the underworld.

Etna A volcanic mountain in Sicily.

Etruria Region north of Latium in Italy where Etruscans live.

Etruscans Also called Tuscans. People who live in Etruria and who become allies of Aeneas in effort to overthrow tyrant Mezentius.

Euryalus Beautiful young man and friend of Nisus.

Eurydice Wife of Orpheus.

Evander Greek king who founded city at Pallanteum, the site that would later become Rome. Aeneas visits him and gets help in Book VIII.

Faunus Old Italian god of woods and agriculture.

Furies Ferocious, avenging goddesses. Allecto is a Fury.

Golden Bough Mythical symbol of immortality. Aeneas must obtain it before he can enter the underworld and be sure of coming out alive.

Hades Name for the underworld.

Harpies Half-bird, half-woman creatures who drive the Trojans off the Strophades islands in Book III.

Hector Trojan hero and son of King Priam who dies defending Troy. Achilles dragged his body around the walls of Troy.

Hecuba Priam's wife and Queen of Troy.

Helen Spartan woman, married to Menelaus, who was seduced by (or eloped with) Paris, a Trojan, and thus caused the Trojan War.

Helenus Son of Priam. He later marries Hector's widow Andromache and settles at Buthrotum, where Aeneas meets him.

Hercules A Greek and Roman hero, renowned for his phenomenal strength.

Hesperia Another name for Italy.

Iarbas King of Mauretania and one of Dido's rejected suitors.

Ida Mountain near Troy.

Idomenius King of Crete and ally of Trojans in Trojan War.

Ilioneus Old and wise Trojan leader.

Ilium Another name for Troy.

Iris Messenger of Juno.

Ithaca Island off west coast of Greece and home of Ulysses.

Iulus Another name for Ascanius.

Janus Two-headed god of the Romans. The opening of the doors of his temple symbolized the beginning of war.

Juno A goddess married to Jupiter, king of the gods. Furious at Trojans.

Jupiter King of the gods.

Juturna A nymph, sister of Turnus.

Labyrinth Built by Daedalus for the minotaur in Crete.

Laocoön Priest of Apollo and Neptune who is killed by serpents at Troy when he warns against the Trojan horse.

Laomedon One of the founders of Troy.

Latins Natives of Latium in Italy.

Latinus King of the Latins.

Latium Plain of west and central Italy where Aeneas fights to build his city.

Latona Mother of Apollo and Diana.

Laurentium Capital of Latium.

Lausus Son of Mezentius, who is killed by Aeneas.

Lavinia Daughter of king Latinus who had been engaged to Turnus, but who is destined to marry Aeneas.

Lavinium City that Aeneas will build.

Lethe One of the rivers of the underworld.

Marcellus Son-in-law of Augustus, who died very young. Mentioned in Book VI in parade of great Romans.

Mars Roman god of war.

Menelaus Helen's husband and leader of Sparta. One of the Greek warriors at Troy.

Mercury Jupiter's messenger.

Mezentius Tyrant who ruled the Etruscans. Killed by Aeneas.

Minerva Jupiter's daughter. Roman goddess of the arts.

Misenus Comrade of Aeneas who was drowned and must be buried before Aeneas can descend to underworld.

Muses Nine goddesses of poetry, music, and the arts.

Nautes Old Trojan sailor who gives Aeneas good advice in Book V.

Neoptolemus Another name of Pyrrhus.

Neptune God of the sea.

Nereids Sea nymphs.

Nisus Young Trojan who is a loyal friend to Euryalus.

Numa Second king of early Rome.

Nymphs Minor deities.

Octavian Augustus' family name and the name he used before he was given the title Augustus.

Odysseus Greek name for Ulysses.

Olympus Mountain in northern Greece where the gods supposedly lived.

Orpheus A poet and musician who visited the underworld to try to resurrect his wife.

Palinurus Aeneas' pilot who falls overboard just before the Trojans reach Italy.

Pallanteum Evander's city in Italy and the site of Rome.

Pallas Evander's son, who is killed by Turnus.

Panthus Trojan priest who brings Trojan gods to Aeneas when Troy falls.

Paris Trojan prince whose affair with Helen causes the Trojan War.

Pasiphae Wife of Minos and queen of Crete who fell in love with a bull and gave birth to the minotaur.

Penates Protecting gods of the household, which Aeneas carries out of Troy.

Pergama Another name for Troy.

Phoenicians People from eastern Mediterranean who settle in Carthage.

Polydorus Son of Priam, who was murdered in Thrace. His ghost speaks to Aeneas in Book III.

Polyphemus One of the Cyclopes who was blinded by Ulysses and who tries to attack the Trojans.

Prometheus A Titan who gave fire to man.

Proserpina Queen of the underworld.

Proteus Sea god who helped Neptune.

Pygmalion King of Tyre and Dido's brother who murdered her husband, Sychaeus, for his money.

Pyrrhus A son of Achilles who brutally kills King Priam and his son.

Quirinus Ancient Roman deity.

Remus Twin brother of Romulus.

Romulus Founder and first king of Rome. Son of Mars and descendant of Aeneas.

Rutulians Tribe in Latium led by Turnus.

Saturn Old Italian god.

Scylla A monster who devoured sailors in the strait between Italy and Sicily.

Sibyl Prophetess inspired by Apollo. She leads Aeneas to the underworld. Also called Deiphobe.

Sidon City of Phoenicia.

Sinon Greek spy who convinced the Trojans to bring the Trojan Horse inside the walls of Troy.

Sirens Creatures who lure sailors to their deaths.

Strophades Islands off west coast of Greece where Trojans are attacked by Harpies.

Styx One of the rivers of the underworld.

Sychaeus Husband of Dido, who was murdered by Dido's brother.

Tarchon   Etruscan king and ally of Aeneas.

Tarquin   Name of Etruscan kings.

Tartarus   The part of the underworld where wicked shades were punished.

Tenedos   An island off the coast of Troy where the Greeks hide before they attack Troy.

Thrace   A region just north of Troy.

Tiber   River that runs through Rome.

Turnus   Chief of the Rutulians and Aeneas' major enemy in Latium. Killed by Aeneas.

Tyre   Phoenician city.

Tyrrhenian Sea   Part of the Mediterranean that touches the west coast of Italy.

Ulysses   Greek hero who fought in Trojan War and who is the subject of the *Odyssey*, in which his ten-year effort to get home is described.

Venus   Goddess of love and Aeneas' mother.

Vesta   Roman goddess of the hearth.

Volscians   A tribe in Italy, hostile to the Trojans.

Vulcan   Venus' husband and smith of the gods. He makes armor for Aeneas.

The Critics

The Price of Success

If, then, the *Aeneid* is a story of success, it is also a story of what success costs: the cost to the land, the cost in lives—and it is characteristic of Virgil that we should remember not the victors but the defeated, Camilla, Nisus and Euryalus, Pallas, Lausus, Turnus, even Mezentius . . . —and, finally, the cost to Aeneas himself. He is reborn, to be sure, as the ideal Roman incarnate, but by this very fact he becomes increasingly isolated from any human contact. He loses his wife, his father, even his nurse Caieta; the only human relationship he is allowed is with his son, and that seems less personal than dynastic.

> *Steele Commager, ed., "Introduction" to* Virgil, Collection of Critical Essays, *1966*

Unlike Homer's heroes, the figure of Aeneas simultaneously comprises past, present, and future. . . . In the *Aeneid* we see for the first time the tragedy of man suffering from historical fate. The hero is never allowed to belong completely to the moment. If and when, as in Carthage, he seems to be caught up in the moment, a god reminds him of his duty.

> *Viktor Poschl,* The Art of Vergil, *1962*

The *Aeneid* as the Story of Rome

The real subject of the *Aeneid* is not Aeneas . . . it is Rome and the glories of her empire, seen as the romanticist sees the great past. The first title given it was *The Deeds of the Roman People*. Aeneas is important because he carries Rome's destiny; he is to be her founder by the high decrees of fate.

> *Edith Hamilton,* The Roman Way, *1960*

Virgil owed his immediate acceptance as the prince of Latin poets, and still owes his place among the supreme poets of the world, not merely to his insight into the life of man and nature, his majesty and tenderness, and the melodious perfection of his verse. Over and above all these, he was the interpreter, we may even call him the creator, of a great national ideal. That ideal was at once political, social and religious. The supremacy of Rome took in his hands the aspect of an ordinance of Providence, towards which all previous history had been leading up under divine guidance. It meant the establishment of an empire to which no limit of time or space was set, and in which the human race would find ordered peace, settled government, material prosperity, the reign of law and the commonwealth of freedom.

> *J. W. Mackail*, Virgil and His
> Meaning To The World of Today,
> *1963*

Each detail of the *Aeneid* is drenched with symbolism and . . . it must be read at several levels. But the symbolism of the sum is simple. An inevitable civil war—all the participants were Italians, all ancestors of the Romans—had happily come to its period. All had fought well and, according to their best lights, justly. All bitterness and all passion was now laid at rest, and all could now join hands as comrades and together walk to meet the shining future.

> *Moses Hadas*, A History of Latin
> Literature, *1952*

The Triumph of Order Over Disorder

The struggle and final victory of order—this subduing of the demonic which is the basic theme of the poem, appears and reappears in many variations. The demonic appears in history as civil or foreign war, in the soul as passion, and in nature as death and destruction. Jupiter, Aeneas, and Augustus are its conquerors, while Juno, Dido, Turnus, and Antony are its conquered representatives. The contrast between Jupiter's powerful composure and Juno's confused passion reappears in the contrast between Aeneas and Dido and between Aeneas and Turnus.

> *Viktor Poschl*, The Art of Vergil, *1962*

The Characters and Their Drama

In the first place Aeneas is a hero in search of his soul. The *Aeneid* is very much of a spiritual quest, which makes it unique in ancient literature. Only Virgil admits of the possibility that a character can change, grow and develop. Aeneas in the early books is unsure of himself, always seeking instructions from his father or from the gods before committing himself to any course of action. In the underworld he sees a panorama of the future history of Rome down to the time of Augustus, and that vision gives him the self-confidence to act on his own initiative.

> *R. M. Ogilvie*, Roman Literature and Society, *1980*

Virgil could do a great love story. Aeneas and Dido are not only the hero and heroine of our very first romance, they are great lovers, too, the woman the greater, as through the ages the poets have loved to portray her. She is 'Pierced by love's cruel shaft, feeding the wound with her life-blood and wasting under a hidden fire'; if she is with him 'she begins to speak and stops midway in the utterance'; he speaks and 'she hangs upon his lips.' When the night comes and the banquet hall is empty, she steals there from her bed to find the couch he had lain on and stretch herself upon it.

> *Edith Hamilton*, The Roman Way, *1960*

Vergil, I think, has caught a truth in this representation of angry, murderous Aeneas. Killing Turnus is a victory for the cause, but not for Aeneas. In this final struggle . . . Aeneas can only be the loser. Triumphant he should never be; angry, I feel that I understand him better. It is his final assertion against (enslavement to?) the destiny that has almost dehumanized him, the final proof by Vergil that "pius Aeneas" (pious Aeneas) is not passive, but more tragic than Dido and Turnus together.

> *William S. Anderson*, The Art of the Aeneid, *1969*